The
Apostle Peter
Speaks to Us
Today

The Apostle Peter Speaks To Us Today

HOLMES ROLSTON

JOHN KNOX PRESS
ATLANTA

Library of Congress Cataloging in Publication Data

Rolston, Holmes, 1900-
The Apostle Peter speaks to us today.

1. Bible. N.T. 1 Peter—Sermons. 2. Presbyterian Church—Sermons. 3. Sermons, American. I. Title.
BS2795.4.R64   227'.92'07   76-44974   ISBN 0-8042-0201-X

Dedication

When I was pastor of the West Avenue Presbyterian Church in Charlotte, North Carolina, I held in this church a series of pre-Easter services based on First Peter. Dr. Hunter Blakely, who at the time was President of Queens College in Charlotte, had told me that in his opinion the best commentary on First Peter was by Selwyn in the Macmillan Series. I borrowed his copy and told my people that I was basing much of what I was telling them on this book.

Shortly after the conclusion of these services I held a funeral service for a member of this church who had attended the Easter services. In appreciation I received as a gift a copy of this book from his wife. When I left the pastorate of this church about a year and a half later, I received a gift copy of the same book from a couple I had been able to lead back into an active life in the church. They also had attended the Easter services.

When Robert F. Boyd, who had been pastor of the Saint Andrews Presbyterian Church in Charlotte, came to Richmond to teach the Bible in the Presbyterian School of Christian Education, I found out that he did not have a copy of this commentary. I gave him one of my copies, clipping out the page of dedication and putting it in my other copy. He used the copy I had given him as he taught First Peter to his students. He agreed with me and with Hunter Blakely that Selwyn had written the best commentary on First Peter.

It has seemed appropriate therefore for me to dedicate these expositions of the message of First Peter to my friend, Robert F. Boyd, who is at present pastor of the Crestwood Presbyterian Church of Richmond, Virginia. He and I would also agree that the task of the expositor or teacher of a book of the Bible is to hear the message that the original writer intended to convey to his readers and to express that message without distortion of its meaning in its relevance to the lives of those who must live their Christian life in the context of our contemporary world.

—Holmes Rolston

Contents

Introduction

This manuscript has grown out of studies I have made of First Peter. At various times I have based a series of pre-Easter studies on this epistle. In my regular preaching I have frequently preached sermons on selected texts or on longer passages from this letter. I have no intention to attempt to compete with the great commentaries that have already been written on First Peter. I have in my possession a number of these. The two most important of the commentaries I have are *The First Epistle of St. Peter* by Edward Gordon Selwyn in the Macmillan Series, and *St. Peter and St. Jude* by Bigg in the International Critical Commentary Series, published by Scribner's. I have used most frequently in my study the first of these. I consider this to be the great commentary on First Peter. I have also *The Epistle of St. Peter* by Lumby in the *Expositor's Bible* and *St. Peter and St. Jude* by Plumptre in *The Cambridge Bible for Schools and Colleges.* Among the briefer treatments I have Erdman in *The General Epistles* and John W. Bowman in volume 24 of the *Layman's Bible Commentary.*

The great critical commentaries are written for serious students who have the knowledge of the Greek language to follow discussions of the structure of Greek sentences and the various meanings of Greek words. I am writing to preachers who in the midst of their various activities in their work as pastors are looking for suggestions that they may develop into sermons without distorting the true meaning of the passage they are studying. I am writing also to adults who wish to come to a fresh understanding in the life of our world today of the message of the New Testament and to the knowledge of the will of God for them in their own peculiar life situations.

Books of sermons based on the letters of Peter have been written. Two of these are in my library. One of them is by

Jowett and is made up of sermons preached by him when he was pastor of the Fifth Avenue Presbyterian Church of New York. My copy was given to my father in 1914. This is an able volume from one of the greatest preachers of his generation. There is much in it that is of permanent value. But Jowett speaks to the issues of his time, and the book would not be available to many people today. An even older book is a volume of *The Sermon Bible* which covers the books of the New Testament from First Peter to Revelation. The method of treatment is to bring together excerpts from sermons that have been preached on these books. The book would not be known by many people today. (In this time of inflation it is interesting to observe that the eight volumes on the New Testament prepaid by post or express were for sale for nine dollars.)

Without underestimating the significance of other books of the New Testament we can say that First Peter is a very important book for those who would understand the basic content of the witness of the writers of the New Testament to the Christian faith and the relevance of this faith to the crucial issues of life today. This importance roots in our knowledge of the central place of Peter in the events of history which are associated with the beginning of the Christian faith. This importance is illustrated by the fact that there has been published in 1973 a book entitled *Peter in the New Testament*. It is edited by Raymond E. Brown and others and is published jointly by the Augsburg Publishing House (Lutheran) and the Paulist Press (Roman Catholic). The book is produced by an ecumenical array of scholars drawn from both Protestant and Catholic backgrounds to emphasize the thinking concerning Peter in which these scholars can agree and to serve as a background for ecumenical discussions of The Role of the Papacy in the Universal Church. The publication of this book is evidence of the ecumenical discussions going on between Catholics and Protestants today that would not have been possible before the Second Vatican Council. But it is also a proof of the abiding significance of Peter for those who would seek to understand his importance for a community of believing Christians in which both Catholics and Protestants are seeking to find their place. All Christians are agreed that Peter was closely associated with Jesus in the days of his flesh as the leader and spokesman of the band of disciples which he was training. Peter is also the central figure in the story of the beginnings of Christianity in the first part of the Book of Acts.

Peter is the author of the letter to which we refer when we say First Peter. As in this study we are dealing exclusively with First Peter, we are not discussing the authorship of Second Peter. It is fair to say that the majority of New Testament scholars today are uncertain as to its authorship. Selwyn does not accept it as written by Peter. But Bigg does. In his discussion of this matter in *The Layman's Bible Commentary*, John W. Bowman says that we do not at present have the information either to prove that Peter wrote Second Peter or to prove that he did not (see page 160). I would agree with this position. There are certainly some scholars who hold that the author of First Peter was an anonymous Christian who lived during the reign either of Domitian (81-96 A.D.) or Trajan (98-117 A.D.). The language and developed ideas are thus felt to suggest a later date. However, we do hold that the balance of the evidence still offers a reasonable case for an early date and a less remote and secondhand link of the basic material of the letter to Peter.

In discussing the authenticity of the First Epistle of Peter, Bigg writes: "Eusebius places the First Epistle of Peter among the books which were accepted by the whole Church without any feeling of doubt." He continues, "There is no book in the New Testament which has earlier, better, or stronger attestation" (page 7). In his commentary, Bigg devotes pages 7-14 to quotations and references to First Peter in early Christian writings.

When we say that there is reason for confidence about the authenticity of First Peter, we do not mean that all of the letter in the form in which we have it now was written by Peter. Peter himself in the close of his letter tells us that he has used Silvanus, whom he describes as "a faithful brother," as the writer of the epistle. New Testament scholars are consistently agreed that the reference here is to Silas who accompanied Paul as his close companion after Paul separated from Barnabas. There is no way of distinguishing between the work of Peter and the work of Silas in producing the letter which we now know as First Peter. But we can reckon that Peter gave his approval to the letter we have as containing a satisfactory statement of the message which he wished to communicate to the churches to which he was sending it. At the least, we can regard the letter as expressing the authentic teaching of the Apostle. In this study we will thus take the latitude that is reasonable and refer to the author simply as Peter.

The question of the date of the letter is inevitably tied into the question of its authorship. And this question is closely related to our convictions as to the time and place of Peter's death. The probability is that Peter perished in the Neronian persecutions which began in the latter part of 64 A.D. Selwyn, after a long and able discussion of the whole matter, sets the date of the epistle as written in 63 A.D. or even as late as the first part of 64 A.D. Should the case for a later date and author be persuasive eventually, however, we still believe that the letter will continue to reflect apostolic faith and teachings. In the opening words of his letter, Peter tells us that he writes as an apostle of Jesus Christ. The letter is written by Peter in his authority as one who has been chosen by Jesus Christ and commissioned to bear his message to those who will receive it. In 1 Peter 5:1 he tells us that he writes as one who has been a witness of the sufferings of Christ. And the letter as a whole in many of its details gives us the impression of the writing of a man who has seen and heard in their actual happening the things that Jesus said and did and the things that were done to him. His descriptions of the sufferings of Christ present a point of view somewhat different from that of Paul in this respect.

In his opening statement, Peter tells us that his letter is addressed to the exiles of the Dispersion in Pontus, Galatia, Cappadocia, Asia, and Bithynia. New Testament scholars are generally agreed that Peter has listed five provinces of the Roman Empire in an area which is now a part of the land in Asia which is controlled by Turkey. In his use of the term "dispersion" we naturally think of the same term as it was used to describe the Jews as they were scattered in various parts of the ancient world. But while we cannot miss the connotation of the word, the probability is that Peter as he uses it is thinking not of the Jews in their dispersion but of communities of Christians as they were found in the area to which he was sending his letter. These believing communities would unquestionably have included both Jews and Gentiles. It would be a good guess that the majority of the members of most of these communities of Christians were of Gentile origin. But we do not have the information to prove this. The crucial issue which Paul had with the Judaizers among the Galatian Christians which comes to white heat in the letter to the Galatians does not emerge in First Peter. Peter describes his readers as "chosen and destined by God the Father and sanctified by the Spirit for obedience to Jesus Christ and for sprinkling with his blood" (1:2). We have here a very high conception of the Christians as brought into being by and sanctified by the working of the Spirit in their hearts so that they can live in obedience to Jesus Christ. There is also here in the beginning an emphasis on the atoning death of the Christ.

The Christians to whom Peter is writing are exiles in that they know that they share a common faith which is not the dominant faith of the Graeco-Roman world in which they must live. The deepest roots of their lives are in that which God has done for them in Christ. They know that they must live in obedience to their faith in Christ and that at the same time they must live in the world of which they are irrevocably a part. It is in this setting that they must seek to understand the will of Christ for them in the day by day decisions they must make. We have here a pattern of living which is in some ways similar to the way in which Christians today must live in a highly secularized world which does not fully share their basic assumptions as to the meaning and purpose of our human existence. We do not know whether Peter has actually worked in or even visited any of these churches. The letter contains no personal references. But he would of course be known to them for his place of leadership in the Christian community.

When Peter wrote First Peter, he gave expression to his understanding of the Christian faith and his understanding of the implications of this faith for the life of man. In the full movement of the letter he expresses himself on many things. But his central purpose in the writing of the letter is not to give an exposition of the Christian faith. His plan is to write to the Christians in an area in which he feels they are soon to experience persecutions and to enable them to understand themselves and their sufferings in the light of their knowledge of the significance of the suffering and death of Christ. As he writes he speaks of many things, and the things he says on the various subjects that come to his mind are important to us today. But he returns again and again to the theme of the sufferings of Christians in the light of the suffering and death of the Christ for them. In speaking to this theme he speaks also to the needs of Christians today as they are facing suffering and persecution.

Peter as he writes First Peter reveals himself as a man who is profoundly rooted in the Old Testament. If the reader would have a firsthand experience of this, it is suggested that he read through this epistle in a copy of the Revised Standard Version. If as he reads he will take time to look up all of the references to the Old Testament which are given at the bottom of the page in connection with the passages he is reading, he is certain to be impressed with the frequency with which Peter refers to the Old Testament in the five chapters of this letter. The translation of the Old Testament with which Peter is most familiar is the Greek Septuagint. This is true of most of the other writers of the New Testament. Peter also quotes very frequently from the Old Testament in the sermons which Luke preserves for us in Acts.

While Peter often quotes the language of the Old Testament, he consistently breathes into its words the Christian concepts which he is seeking to proclaim. Peter was convinced that the faith he was preaching was the true development of the revelation that he found preserved for him in the Old Testament. We can be confident that he was sure that it was only in the light of the knowledge of what God had done for man in Jesus Christ that the Old Testament was to be fully understood. He deals with the Old Testament in its relation to Jesus Christ in chapter 1, verses 10-12. He was convinced that the Judaism in which he had been nurtured missed its great opportunity when the Jews who were contemporary with his generation rejected the witness of the Christians to Jesus Christ as the true Messiah of Israel.

Peter, as he writes to those whom he calls the exiles of the dispersion, is fully committed to the pattern in which the message of that which God has done for man in Christ is proclaimed as a way of salvation to every human being who will receive it. He is also committed to the conviction that those who respond in repentence, love, faith, and obedience to the message of the gospel are to be received into the fellowship of the Christian community of faith without any distinctions based on the distinctions of race, class, and nation, as they are to be found in the secular world in which the Christians must live.

The crucial break through to the Gentile world which was involved in the baptism into the Christian church of Cornelius and his friends at Caesarea came through Peter. Peter acted here in obedience to what he considered a special revelation of the Holy Spirit.

Of course the full implementation of this insight of the universality of the Christian faith was wrought out in the ministry of Paul as the apostle to the Gentiles. On this issue Paul and Peter stood together over against those who wished to compel the Gentiles to receive circumcision and keep the law of Moses. But the issue which was so urgent in church at the time that Paul wrote the letter to the Galatians had probably been fully accepted in the Gentile church when Peter wrote his epistle.

Some students of First Peter feel that Peter was probably familiar with some of the writings of Paul when he wrote his letter. And Silas, who probably did much of the actual writing of the letter, had been intimately associated with Paul.

In the close of his letter, Peter refers to Mark and calls him his son (5:13). Mark was closely associated with Peter. Papias, writing about 140 A.D. but basing his comments on earlier material known to him, writes: "Mark, having become Peter's interpreter, wrote down accurately. . . as many as he remembered of the things said and done by the Lord." (*The Westminster Dictionary of the Bible*, page 376). The setting in which this statement is found shows clearly that Papias is referring to the sayings of Peter as preserved by Mark. Most scholars feel that the Gospel of Mark was the first of the gospels to be written. We are thus perhaps indebted to Peter's preaching as remembered by Mark for our first account of the words and deeds of Jesus in the days of his flesh. If this interpretation is true, we could be ultimately indebted to Peter for much that we know today about Jesus.

Our basic concern here is with First Peter. If we have in this letter an authentic epistle written by Peter toward the close of his life to the Christians in Asia Minor, we have a priceless document. It is our purpose to seek to hear and understand the message that Peter meant to give to his readers. But it is also our purpose to go beyond this and ask what the things that are said here mean to us in the context of the world we live in. We will not have really heard this message unless we discover in it an element of confrontation in which the One who sent Peter confronts us and we seek to ask what the will of the Christ is for us today.

As Bultmann brings his *Theology of the New Testament* to a close he writes: "It is of decisive importance that the theological thoughts be conceived and explicated as thoughts of faith, that is as thoughts in which faith's understanding of God, the world, and man is unfolding itself—not as products of free speculation or of a scientific mastering of 'God,' 'the world' and 'man' carried out by the objectifying kind of thinking" (p. 237).

We do not have to follow Bultmann in all of his thinking to realize the truth of what he is saying here. Christians who have heard the Word of God in Christ and responded to it must start from the central convictions of their faith as they seek to live in a world that is very different from the world in which the New

Testament writers lived. We do not live on a flat earth with heaven above and hell below. We do not live in the comparatively simple world of the first century. We live in a world of science and in a highly developed industrial society where it is not always easy to take the thoughts of the New Testament and develop from them an understanding of life in our own concrete situation. But if we are to come to know the will of God for us in our life situation it is important for us to have first heard the word of faith spoken by Peter to the exiles of the dispersion in their life situation as he understood it.

This study of First Peter will follow the movement of the letter as a whole. The weakness of this type of treatment is that it does not give adequate opportunity for detailed comment on all of the various verses of the text. The text of First Peter contains more verses that are suitable for reflection and study than many other portions of the New Testament of similar length. The advantage of this approach, however, is that we are helped to hear what Peter has said concerning the content of the Christian faith and to follow the way in which he relates his thought to the life situations of his readers. We can hear his emphasis on the possibility and the necessity for each individual reader to work out the meaning of faith for himself and to discern the will of Christ in his own particular situation amid the various alternatives that are possible for him.

The thought of Peter as expressed in his letter to the Christians in Asia and in his speeches in Acts fits perfectly into the point of view of the much larger study of the Christian faith in its relation to the issues of our time expressed in *The Common Catechism*. Translated from the German and published in English in 1973, this book contains the efforts of forty Protestant and Roman Catholic scholars to give a statement of the Christian faith in the context of the great questions of our contemporary world. First Peter displays this same sensitivity to the critical problems of life, and for this reason the author seems to speak realistically to us.

For a brief but cogent summary of recent critical scholarship on 1 Peter, the reader is advised to consult the volume on 1 and 2 Peter, etc., in the Proclamation Commentaries Series, edited by Gerhard Krodel and published by Fortress Press. Our approach differs, however, not with respect to concern for scholarship but with the intention of providing an introduction to the early Christian faith that developed around one letter and which was traditionally expressed within it.

1
The Significance
of the Resurrection

"Born anew to a living hope through
the resurrection of Jesus Christ from the
dead." 1 Peter 1:3

Scripture Background: 1 Peter 1:3-5

The passage we are considering begins with a doxology: "Blessed be the God and Father of our Lord Jesus Christ." This doxology points backward to verse 2 where the reference is to the church as chosen by God and sanctified by the Spirit to obedience to Jesus Christ. In harmony with the central theme of the epistle there is a reference to the atonement wrought out by his death. While the doctrine of the one God in three persons is not developed in this verse, it underlies the thought. But the doxology points forward to what God has done for the new community of faith through the resurrection of Jesus Christ from the dead.

The affirmation of the passage is that God has brought the Christians to a living hope of the life for them that lies beyond death. It is interesting to observe that Peter does not at any place in his first epistle attempt to establish the fact of the resurrection of Jesus Christ from the dead. He assumes this as a conviction that is common to him and his readers that does not need to be established.

There is a sense in which this is a strong argument for the belief that the resurrection of Jesus Christ from the dead was an event which actually happened in the context of the events of history as we know it. Of course it has implications that go far beyond the context of history. But the Christian faith is rooted in history.

It is difficult to think of a man better prepared than Peter to give his witness to the reality of the resurrection. According to John, he was the first of the apostles to enter the empty tomb (John 20:6). And Luke reports that when Cleopas and his companion are hastening back from Emmaus to give to the disciples their witness to their encounter with the risen Lord, they are met by the apostles who say to them, "The Lord has risen indeed, and has appeared unto Simon" (Luke 24:34). Paul confirms this when he says that the third day Jesus appeared to Cephas (1 Cor. 15:5). The New Testament witness is that Peter was with the other disciples in the various times when Jesus presented himself alive to his disciples (Acts 1:2). Peter was the spokesman for the apostles when he gave the witness to the resurrection on the day of Pentecost (Acts 2:32). In his speech to a Gentile audience in the home of Cornelius, Peter says of Jesus: "God raised him on the third day and made him manifest; not to all the people but to us who were chosen by God as witnesses, who ate and drank with him after he rose from the dead (Acts 10:40-41). And special attention should be called to John, chapter 21, in which Peter receives forgiveness for his weakness in the time of his denial and is charged to assume his responsibility as the one whom Jesus has commanded to feed his sheep. It could be that Peter writes his letter to those whom he calls exiles in five provinces of Asia as part of his obedience to this command. And when Peter speaks through his letter to those who might be considered exiles in the secular world of today, he could be still fulfilling his responsibility to feed the church of God.

The hope for some form of survival after death is not peculiar to the Christian faith. The Greek philosphers came to the belief in the possibility of the immortality of the soul. The Pharisees who were contemporary with Jesus believed in the resurrection of the dead. This was a point of debate between the Pharisees and the Sadducees. (See Acts 23:6-10 for a vivid illustration of this difference.) Peter affirms that when God brought again Jesus Christ from the dead he gave to the community of those who were

to become the followers of Jesus a vital hope that went beyond
the hope of victory over death that was to be found among the
Jews or the Greeks or anywhere in the non-Christian world.

The proclamation of the Christian faith is rooted in the hope
of the resurrection. We must understand of course that the
Christian witness to the resurrection went beyond the idea of a
resuscitation. Jesus brought Lazarus back from death. But death
for Lazarus was postponed, not conquered. Christians believed
in the witness to the empty tomb. But Cleopas and his friend
could be aware of the empty tomb without believing in the
living Lord (Luke 24:24). The faith of the followers of Jesus was
rooted in their belief that the living Lord had manifested himself
as alive after his death to "the apostles whom he had chosen"
(Acts 1:2).

Peter's concern as he writes his letter is with the meaning of
the witness to the resurrection of Jesus in the life of the community of faith. He says that Christians through their belief in what
God had done for them in Christ have been born anew to "an
inheritance which is imperishable, and undefiled, and unfading,"
and that this inheritance is kept in heaven for them. The inheritance which was the hope of the Christian exiles of the dispersion is described here in terms of the negation of life in this
present world. It involves the removal of the critical limitations
in the life we know now. The first of these is simply the brevity of
life. Life within the world we know is marked by existence unto
death. In the 90th Psalm we read: "The years of our life are
threescore and ten, or even by reason of strength fourscore." The
psalmist adds, "Yet their span is but toil and trouble; they are
soon gone, and we fly away" (verse 10). But the Christian
inheritance of which Peter speaks is an everlasting inheritance.
It is also undefiled. The second limitation is that the life which we
know in this present world is marked by the presence of evil.
This affects the life of society as a whole. We live in a world in
which there are many who walk in the way of evil. And those
who seek to be obedient to the Christ are fully aware that they
do not achieve complete victory over evil. But they hope for a

world which will be a world without sin. The word "unfailing"
does in a sense lift again the concept of imperishable. But there
is a sense in which the life we know on earth is marked by the
element of decay apart from its association with the element of
evil. This is the third limitation. As people grow older they will
in time come to the place at which they have to realize that their
physical strength is no longer with them. They may experience
inner renewal, but often both mental and physical powers break
down. In this situation they look for a heritage in which the
element of decay has passed away.

We should not describe the heritage of the children of God
in purely negative terms. As Paul in the close of the 13th chapter
of First Corinthians describes the passage from this world to the
resurrection world of God, he says: "So faith, hope, love abide,
these three; but the greatest of these is love" (verse 13). It is
the conviction of Christians that their inheritance also involves
a possibility of communion with the living Lord which go beyond the experiences of communion with him which they can
know in their earthly life. (See Philippians 1:23.)

Peter tells his readers that this inheritance is kept in heaven
for them. Peter could use the word "heaven" without further explanation because he lived in a world where it was not difficult for
him and his readers to think of heaven as above the earth. We
live in a world of space travel in which we have to rethink our
basic concepts of the universe. But Peter and the apostles had
seen in the context of life in this world the Lord's manifestation
of himself in such a way that he bore effective witness to the
reality of the resurrection world of God that lies beyond the life
we know in this world.

Our passage combines both the consciousness of an inheritance
kept in heaven for the children of God and the looking for a
salvation that "is ready to be revealed at the last time." Peter's
epistle is not dominated by the expectation of the return of
Christ in the near future in the way that this expectation dominates Paul's first letter to the Thessalonians. When Peter writes
more than a decade has passed since Paul wrote to the Thessalon-

ians, and the sense of immediate urgency cannot endure forever. But Peter shares the thought of a consummation which is to mark the end of time as we know it. He would remind the secularists of our age of the witness of the apostles to the reality of the resurrection world of God that confronts us in Jesus Christ.

2
Suffering Various Trials

"Now for a little while you may have to
suffer various trials." 1 Peter 1:6

Scripture Background: 1 Peter 1:6-7

The background of these verses is the hope that Christians have of a salvation that will be revealed at the last time, whether this is for them death or the consummation of God's redemption in the second coming of the Christ. Those who have this hope rejoice in it.

But Peter writes as a realist. He knows that the Christians in the churches of Asia to which his letter is to be sent are living in a world which is in the main hostile to their faith. And he knows that these Christians before they enter into the glory of their Lord will be called upon to suffer various trials. When Peter speaks of *various* trials, he makes it possible for us to include in the things we are thinking of the many different kinds of trials that could come to people in the time in which Peter lived and also the very different kinds of testing which Christians may face in the various situations in which they may find themselves in the complex industrial society of today. As we think of the various trials we can properly think of those that go with our physical well-being including the suffering that is often involved in sickness and in the inevitable disintegration of the human body which comes with advancing age. We can think also of the way in which people suffer as they come into contact with the evil of our world. We can think also of the suffering that is brought about through famine and war. In our time men have developed instruments of destruction that were unknown in the ancient world. And the threat of thermonuclear destruction hangs over the whole of our contemporary civilization.

But the probability is that Peter as he writes this letter is thinking primarily of the sufferings that Christians would face because of their loyalty to their faith in the context of a hostile world. We have seen in the Introduction that Selwyn prefers to date First Peter as written probably in Rome at a time not too long before the beginning of the Neronian persecution in the latter part of 64 A.D. If this is correct Peter must have been sensitive to the growing opposition to the Christian faith in Rome. And his awareness of the situation in Rome would indicate that he was conscious of similar situations for the churches of Asia.

It is interesting to observe that in this first reference to the suffering of Christians in his letter Peter does not make a specific reference to the sufferings of Christ. Running through the letter as a whole there is the effort to get the Christians in Asia to see their sufferings in the light of the sufferings of Christ. And this cannot have been completely out of his mind as he makes this initial reference to suffering. The thought of what God has done for them in Christ is present as he asks Christians to face their sufferings in the light of the glory that is to come and as he contrasts the brevity of the sufferings we will face in this world with the permanence of the inheritance they are to receive.

In the verses which are before us, Peter tells us that the genuineness of our faith is tested by the way in which we suffer the various trials that come to us. He uses the familiar example of the way precious metals such as silver and gold are purified by being subjected to intense heat which destroys the impurities in the ore in which they are found. He says that these precious metals which are purified by heating still belong to a perishable world and that they are not to be compared to the faith of a Christian which has been tested in the furnace of affliction and proved to be genuine. And he urges his readers so to live that when they stand before Jesus Christ they will receive from him praise and glory and honor. Peter is in harmony here with the teaching of the letter to the Hebrews, chapter 12:1-11, the letter of James, the brother of our Lord, chapter 1, verse 12, and of Paul in Romans, chapter 5, verse 3. We must not take the element of struggle and discipline out of our Christian life. Browning has put this thought in the words of Rabbi Ezra when he has him say:

> Then, welcome each rebuff
> That turns earth's smoothness rough,
> Each sting that bids nor sit nor stand but go!
> Be our joys three-parts pain!
> Strive, and hold cheap the strain;
> Learn, nor account the pang; dare, never grudge the throe!

   (*Browning's Complete Works*, Cambridge Edition, p. 384)

In the context of a secular society, with the sufferings that are encountered, the full treatment of the sufferings of Christians in the light of the sufferings of the Christ for their salvation that is given in other passages in the letter is striking. Some of these passages are 1 Peter 1:19; 2:20-24; 4:12-19 and 5:10. We will examine them in their setting.

As we deal with the message of First Peter as a whole and in particular with the theme of suffering which runs through the letter we should realize that Peter seeks to give his personal witness to the experiences of Jesus in rejection, suffering, and death. He emphasizes the significance of his resurrection, and sets the sufferings of Christians against the background of the sufferings of the Christ.

In this letter, God makes himself known through a Person who comes into the world and lives a life of love and ministry to people. This Person identifies himself with the needs of those who have been rejected by society as a whole. This identification becomes so complete that he is rejected by the society in which he lives. In the end this rejection leads to his death by crucifixion. This Person is conscious of the fact that in moving toward suffering and death he is accomplishing the purpose of the ONE who sent him into the world whom he calls Father. His sense of rejection is complete in the cry on the cross which is preserved for us by Mark: "My God, my God, why has thou forsaken me? (Mark 15:34). Beyond the word of this cry there does come the witness to the resurrection which is given not to all the people but to those who were chosen by God as witnesses (Act 10:41).

If God is revealed by this Person who dies rejected and forsaken, he is revealed as the God who loves the rejected and forsaken enough to send his Son to suffer and die for them. And if the true knowledge of God is found here he is not the unmoved mover of the Greeks who is without the capacity to love and suffer. He is the God who creates human beings in his own image and loves them enough, in spite of their sins and their rejection of him, to send his Son to bear their sins and to die in their place. But if we follow the suffering of the Christ through to the suffering of the Father we must realize that the call to become disciples of Jesus means that we must share with him his compassion for the poor, the hungry, the sinning, and the rejected. And this means that those who would follow Jesus in the midst of our contemporary world must be ready if necessary to enter into the fellowship of his sufferings as they give themselves to the needs of the rejected of their society.

3
Without Having Seen Him
You Love Him

Scripture Background: 1 Peter 1:8-9

The *Him* in our title refers to Jesus Christ. As Peter writes to the Christians in the five Roman provinces of Asia which he names, he points them to a Person whom they have not seen or known in the flesh who is also a Person whom they love. They had come to love deeply a Person whom they had never seen. We may not be able to love a person whom we have never seen in the same way in which we love persons with whom we are constantly associated in our everyday living, but it is possible for us to come to love and trust persons we have never seen.

The Christians in the churches of Asia had come to love Jesus because of the witness to him by the evangelists who bore to them the good news of Jesus Christ. We cannot know the exact form in which the gospel of Jesus Christ was proclaimed to the people of Asia. But as Peter speaks to Cornelius and his friends in Caesarea, he gives us as he is reported by Luke a good summary of the pattern in which the glad tidings of the Christian faith could be proclaimed to people of a Gentile background (Acts 10:37-43). Peter begins, as Mark begins in his gospel based on the preaching of Peter, with the story of the coming of John the Baptist. He passes at once to tell of a person known as Jesus of Nazareth, and he says that God anointed him with the Holy Spirit and with power. He describes the public ministry of Jesus by saying that "he went about doing good and healing all that were oppressed by the devil." He also bears witness to the sense of the presence of God with him in his ministry. He says that Jesus carried on his ministry both in the country of the Jews and in Jerusalem. He tells the story of the rejection of Jesus and of his death by crucifixion as he says: "They put him to death by hanging him on a tree." He gives his testimony to the resurrection when he says: "God raised him on the third day and made him manifest; not to all the people but to us who were chosen by God as witnesses, who ate and drank with him after he rose from the dead." He gives the abiding significance of the story he is telling when he says that "He [the risen Jesus] commanded us to preach to the people and to testify that he is the one ordained by God to be the judge of the living and the dead." He gives relevance of the story to the lives of those to whom he is speaking when he says: "To him all the prophets bear witness that everyone who believes in him receives forgiveness of sins through his name."

While this is a very brief summary, we can be sure that it sets forth the substance of the message proclaimed by the Christian evangelists to the people of Asia. The story which is told here points to a unique Person who was rejected by many of his contemporaries because his message cut across their basic convictions and their patterns of living. But the story points to a Person who loved people and a Person to whom those who knew him best responded in love and in trust. Such a Person can be loved and believed in by those who have never seen him.

The story as Peter tells it points to a Person who went about doing good and delivering people from the power of evil. The story particularly in its witness to the resurrection has in it elements of the supernatural and cuts across the accepted experience of the finality of death.

How is it that this story which was received with unbelief and ridicule by many of the people of the ancient world came to be accepted by others who responded in love, faith, and obedience

to the unique Person who is witnessed to in it? In the experience
of Peter at Caesarea, which is not fundamentally different from
the experience of those to whom Peter spoke at Pentecost, God
through the Holy Spirit witnessed in the hearts of those who
heard him to the truth of the story he was telling. And as the
apostles went out in obedience to the commands of Jesus to
give their witness to the Gentile world, they went out in the
expectation that their witness would be accompanied by the
testimony of the Holy Spirit. Paul in writing to the Thessalonians says: "Our gospel came to you not only in word, but also
in power and in the Holy Spirit and with full conviction" (1
Thessalonians 1:5).

It is possible for us to love a Person we have never seen.
As I sit in my study and write, I have before me pictures of
members of my immediate family whom I have known and
loved and from whom I have received love. Much of the rich-
ness and meaning of my life is involved in these experiences.
But there are other pictures. One is a picture by Rembrandt
of Aristotle contemplating a bust of Homer. I value the picture
because it reminds me of how much I and others in our western
civilization owe to the great Greeks. I have also a picture by
Rembrandt of the Apostle Paul writing a letter. This picture
reminds me of how much my life has been molded by the study
of the letters of Paul. Paul in his letters has revealed himself
in such intimacy that I feel that I know and love him. I have
also a picture of Karl Barth, and I can never forget how much
it meant to me when, as a student at New College in Edinburgh,
I began to read the writings of Karl Barth and hear his testimony
to the Word of God as the basis of our knowledge of the God
who confronts us, as he confronted Barth when he tried to write
out his study of Paul's letter to the Romans. But the real significance in my life is not that I have come to know and love
many persons whom I may not have seen in the flesh. The real
impact of Paul and Karl Barth on my life is that they have
pointed me effectively to what God has done for me in Jesus
Christ.

I remember that at one time I was talking to a man who was not a Christian. He said that to him Jesus Christ was just a figure of history even as Robert E. Lee was a figure of history. I could learn much from the example of Robert E. Lee but I could not pray to him. The evangelists who called into being the churches to whom Peter was writing pointed their hearers to a unique Person who had lived and died and been raised from the dead and was alive forever more. Because of this they were able to respond in love to him in his love for them, to believe on him and to trust him for the salvation of their souls.

The reference to those who were able to love a Person whom they had never seen is placed in its setting in First Peter immediately after the passage in which Peter, starting with the reality of the resurrection, has spoken to his readers of the inheritance imperishable, undefiled, and fading not away which is laid up in heaven for them. And in the verses we are studying he tells them that they will receive as the outcome of their faith the salvation of their souls. They have here a hope in which he is confident they will not be disappointed.

It is in this setting that Peter describes the Christians to whom he is writing as those who believe in Jesus and rejoice with unutterable and exalted joy. The basic theme of First Peter is to help Christians who are facing times of testing and suffering to understand their sufferings in the light of the sufferings of Christ for them. But he speaks here of their rejoicing in unutterable and exalted joy. He has touched here upon a mark of the first Christians. They were a people who were to live in the midst of tribulations but were also to have deep and abiding sources of joy. It was this that those who opposed them could not understand in them. Paul and Silas could be beaten and chained in the inner prison, but they could sing praises to God. Paul could write to the Philippians a letter from prison but he could say to them: "Rejoice in the Lord always; again I will say, Rejoice" (Phil. 4:4). He could also write: "And the peace of God, which passes all understanding, will keep your hearts and minds in Christ Jesus" (Phil. 4:7). Peter has received from

Jesus the prediction that the time will come when he will stretch out his hands and be bound and carried where he does not wish to go (John 21:18). But he writes in this letter of the unutterable and exalted joy which should be the mark of all who love and trust and obey Jesus Christ.

It is now nearly two thousand years since Jesus was on our earth in the days of his flesh. There is no living man who has seen him but there are millions who have not seen him but believe on him and trust him with the salvation of their souls. May he give them also in the midst of their tribulations the unutterable and exalted joy which he alone can give!

4

Prophets Predict
the Sufferings of Christ
and the Subsequent Glory

Scripture Background: 1 Peter 1:10-12

In the opening verses of the letter which he writes to the exiles of the dispersion, Peter either by direct statements or by good and necessary implications has set forth much of the content of the Christian faith. In a central theme which appears as a sort of unifying thread in the letter as a whole, he seeks to consider the sufferings which he expects these Christians to face in the light of the suffering and death and resurrection of Jesus.

But in verses ten to twelve of the first chapter of his letter, he seeks to relate the faith which they now have to the Judaism from which it has in part emerged and to the sacred writings in which he and his contemporaries in Judaism and also the devout proselytes among the Gentiles have been nourished. He says that the prophets have laid the foundation for the expectation of the coming of the Messiah. He says also that they have predicted the sufferings of the Christ and his subsequent glory.

There can be no question concerning the fact that the Judaism into which Jesus was born was marked by the expectation of the coming of the Messiah. This expectation was part of the basic background of the generation of Judaism in which Jesus lived. His apostles shared in this expectation of the coming of the Christ. This expectation was common both to the followers of Jesus and to those who became the leaders of the opposition to

him. It was shared also by the Samaritans (John 4:25). When
John came baptizing and calling to repentance because the coming
of the kingdom was near, the priests and the Levites from Jerusalem sent a delegation to ask him "Who are you?" John knew
what they had in mind when he said in reply, "I am not the
Christ" (John 1:19-20). And when Jesus appeared preaching,
teaching, and healing and doing mighty works, the question was
immediately raised as to whether or not he was the Christ.

The question for the generation in which Jesus lived was not
whether or not the Christ would come but when he would come
and the kind of person he would be. The Jews of the first century expected the coming of the Messiah, but they did not expect
the coming of a Messiah who would suffer and die. They looked
forward to a Person who would come in the pattern of David to
deliver his people from their political bondage to Rome. They
expected him to set up a kingdom with its center at Jerusalem, a
kingdom of his own people that would have a significant impact
on the life of the world. They did not associate with the Messiah
the passage of Isaiah that dealt with the Suffering Servant.

Jesus, in contrast, combined the concept of the Messiah as
the deliverer of his people with the prophetic concept of the
Suffering Servant. He knew that it was necessary for him to
suffer and to experience rejection and death if he was to accomplish the mission on which his Father had sent him. This ex-
plains the attitude of Jesus toward the concept of the Christ.
He does not like John repudiate the idea that he is the Christ.
When the Samaritan woman speaks to him of the coming of the
Christ, Jesus says to her: "I who speak to you am he" (John
4:26). But at this time he was far away from the centers of
Jewish life and even his disciples were not with him. Jesus per-
forms mighty works which make men wonder if he could be the
Christ, but he does not publicly use the word "Messiah" because
he knows that he is not the kind of Messiah that his people
are looking for. It is in his discourse with his disciples at Caesarea Philippi as reported for us in Matthew 16:13-20 that Jesus
tells his disciples that he is the Christ. In response to his question

to his   disciples as to who they say that he is, Peter speaks as
the spokesman of the disciples as he says: "You are the Christ,
the Son of the living God" (Matthew 16:16). Jesus approves of
the confession of Peter and says that this insight has come to
Peter as a revelation to him from the Father in heaven. But at
the close of this scene he charges his disciples to tell no one
that he is the Christ. And immediately after this scene, he begins
to explain to his disciples that it is necessary for him to suffer
many things from the leaders of his people and be killed. He
combines this prediction with the statement that on the third day
he will be raised (Matthew 16:21).

The statement of Jesus that he must suffer and die was not
popular with his own disciples. Peter is again the spokesman of
the disciples as he says to Jesus, "God forbid, Lord! This shall
never happen to you" (Matthew 16:22). It is interesting to
observe that Peter, who in this scene finds himself unable to
accept the concept of a suffering and dying Messiah, is the
person who can write in the letter that we are studying that the
prophets were true to the inner meaning of the Old Testament
when they predicted the sufferings of the Christ and his subsequent glory.

When the risen Lord talks with Cleopas and his friend on
the way to Emmaus, Cleopas reveals his knowledge of the
empty tomb, but he and his friend have not come to the belief
that he is alive. The living Lord tells them that it was necessary
that the Christ should suffer these things and to enter into his
glory (Luke 24:26). It is here that Christians and Jews diverge
today in their understanding of the Old Testament. Christians are
convinced that Peter was right in his insistence that the prophets
predicted the suffering of Christ and his subsequent glory. They
are certain that the true development of the testimony of the
Old Testament is to be found in the emergence of the Christian
church as the community of faith, the instrument of God's
redemptive purpose in the world.

The idea of the suffering and death of the Messiah was not
initially popular with the followers of Jesus. They did not begin

to understand it until they saw his sufferings in the light of his subsequent glory and as part of the purpose of the Father in making atonement for the sin of man. But for the concept of a suffering and dying Messiah who was to accomplish a work of redemption in which the offer of salvation through faith was to be made on the same terms to every human being who would receive it was unfamiliar to the Jews, although the details varied, many were committed to the idea of the Messiah as a Son of David who would accomplish the political deliverance of his people. Jesus was rejected by the scribes, the Pharisees, and the Sadducees not because they did not want a Messiah but because he was not the kind of Messiah that they wanted. This was true also of the Jews of the dispersion. When Paul came to Thessalonica he argued from the Scriptures that it was necessary for the Christ to suffer and to rise from the dead. He insisted that the Jesus he was proclaiming unto them was the Christ (Acts 17:3). When the Jews saw that some of the Jews and many of the Greeks were believing his testimony to Jesus, they organized a mob to compel Paul to leave the city.

But the concept of a suffering, dying, and risen Lord was not popular with the Gentiles as the answer to the search for God among the non-Jewish people of the ancient world. Many of the intellectuals among the Gentiles could see no meaning in a religion in which people were called upon to worship a crucified Jew. The opposition to this concept of a crucified God persists in many nominally Christian circles today.

But when we have said these things, we still deeply yearn for the capacity to believe in the God who has manifested his love by sending his Son to die for us. Jesus himself said: "And I, when I am lifted up from the earth, will draw all men to myself." John makes it clear that Jesus is referring here to his death on the cross (John 12: 32-33).

Peter gives his testimony to the sufferings of Christ and his subsequent glory. And in this passage he sets the death of Christ in cosmic relations. He says that angels long to look into the good news that is being proclaimed among men as the Holy

Spirit witnesses in the hearts of men to the apostolic proclamation. In God's redemptive act in sending Jesus Christ to die for sinners and to open to them the possibility of an eternal redemption, there is a revelation of the character of the Father in heaven which is meaningful even to the angels.

5

Pass the Time
of Your
Sojourn in Fear

"Conduct yourselves with fear throughout the time of your exile." 1 Peter 1:17

Scripture Background: 1 Peter 1:13-21

In the opening verses of the first chapter of his letter to the
exiles of the dispersion in the churches of Asia, Peter has set
forth either by direct statement or by good and necessary im-
plication much of the content of the Christian faith. As he moves
on in his letter he begins to speak of the implications of their
faith for their way of life. But as he does this he raises two
significant issues and in his treatment of them adds significantly
to his setting forth of the content of the Christian faith. The
first of these is the thought of Christians as sojourners and exiles
in the context of the society in which they are living. We will
deal with this in this chapter. The second is the understanding of
the community of faith as involving the coming into being of a
people who formerly were not a people but now are God's
people. We will consider this in the next chapter.

A college president who was addressing the entering class of
his institution might say to them: "Friends, you should understand in the beginning that you are here as sojourners. Some of
you will be with us for three years or four. Others who move on
to the study of law or medicine may be with us for a longer
time. But all of you are sojourners. You are not here to stay.
Beyond your time with us there must be the experience of entering into the life of the world that is beyond college. And if you are

to understand your life with us you must never forget that you are sojourners.''

As Peter writes to the Christians in the churches of Asia, he tells them that in the context of the society they are living in they have become strangers and exiles. The real roots of their lives are in the resurrection world of God which has confronted them as the risen Lord made himself known to the witnesses God had chosen. This comes out as in verse thirteen of the first chapter he says to them: "Set your hope fully upon the grace that is coming to you at the revelation of Jesus Christ.'' The reference here is probably to the Christian expectation of the return of Christ. But it could be applied also to the Christian expectation of a confrontation with Christ at the time of death. Jürgen Moltmann, the author of the book *The Crucified God,* is also the author of an earlier book entitled *The Theology of Hope.* In this he insists that Christian theology is the theology of hope. It is the hope of those who have heard and believed the message of the risen Lord. Because they believe that God has raised him from the dead they are confident that he is able to keep his promises. Because of this they think of life in the world in which they are now living as a time of sojourn, a time of preparation for entrance into the resurrection world of God.

Because they believe this, Peter insists that they are not to be conformed to the passions of the days when they knew nothing of Christ. They are to spend the time of their sojourn in responding to the call to holiness. The call to discipleship must be a call to holiness if it comes from Jesus Christ. No one could face the Person who is witnessed to in the New Testament or even the Person who is witnessed to in First Peter without knowing that his call to men involves their commitment to holiness.

Peter insists that Jesus has made it known to those who believe in him that he is the bearer of a call to them from the God who is the Father in heaven who judges every man according to his deeds. And he tells them that if they call on the

God to whom he has pointed them they must pass the time of their sojourn in fear. When Peter says that the Father in heaven judges each person according to his works, he is not repudiating his doctrine of salvation by grace. But he is insisting that the Father in heaven can not be indifferent as to whether or not the salvation he brings to men issues in holiness. We do not distort this picture of God when we remind those who have rejected the salvation which Christ has brought that they must ultimately face the God who judges every man according to his works. Those who know this should pass the time of their sojourn in fear.

Peter strikes an even deeper note when he says that Christians should pass the time of their sojourn in fear because of their knowledge of the costliness of their redemption. He says that they have not been redeemed with perishable things such as gold, or silver, or precious stones but with the precious blood of Christ whom he describes as a lamb without blemish or spot. We should notice that we have here the thought which is consistently in the mind of Peter of the difference between perishable things and the things which are not perishable. The perishable things are the things that belong to the life of the visible world we know. The imperishable are those that pass over into the resurrection world of God. The Christian faith that has been tested by affliction and revealed as genuine is more important than gold that perishes. The suffering and death of Christ for the sin of man belongs to the things that are not perishable. And in the closing verses of the first chapter of his letter the living and abiding nature of the Word of God which has called into being the Christian church is contrasted with the things that belong to the world of the flesh that is to pass away.

In the setting of the passage which we are studying we have a tribute to the Christ. Peter uses the language of Old Testament sacrifice to describe the Christ as "a lamb without blemish or spot." This is an affirmation of his sinlessness. We can think here of the witness of John the Baptist as he points to the Christ and says "Behold, the Lamb of God, who takes away the sin of the world" (John 1:29).

In the same setting, Peter says of Jesus: "He was destined before the foundation of the world but was made manifest at the end of times for your sake" (1 Peter 1:20). This is an affirmation of the eternal pre-existence of the Person whom God has sent to bear the word of salvation to sinning man. When God created man in knowledge, righteousness, and holiness and with dominion over the creatures and also with a limited freedom to hear or refuse to hear the Word of God, he was aware that through such a being there could come into the world sin and evil. But the God who sought our free response willed also to redeem us from sin by sending his Son to die for the sin of man and to open the way for the message of redemption. This purpose which had always been in the heart of God was manifested in the context of our world when God sent his Son to die for us. Those who know of this redemption should pass the time of their sojourn in fear.

In verse 21, the passage we are considering ends as it began in verse 13 with what may properly be called a theology of hope. The salvation which has come to us has come from a source outside of ourselves. It roots in the redemptive purpose of God which has been manifested at a definite time and place in human history. It has been witnessed to us by those who have been chosen of God. Their testimony includes the witness to God's resurrection of the Christ from the dead and the glory of his ascension to the Father in heaven. Through these events which are both in history and beyond history those who have responded to God's offer of salvation in Jesus have a faith and hope in God. They are convinced that the God who has confronted us here is both able and willing to keep his promises. They have a theology of hope.

The concept of their life in the visible world, which we know as a sojourn in which Christians are strangers and exiles in the context of the secular society in which they live, is an essential mark of the community of faith. The pattern of the secular society in which particular Christian communities must live will vary widely in the life of our contemporary world. Some will be living in pagan societies which may be willing to listen to the proclamation of the message of the gospel. Others may live in Marxist societies in which the powers that be are seeking to destroy the Christian faith as an outworn superstition. Some may live in societies which have been deeply penetrated by the insights of the Christian faith. But these are not to be identified with the kingdom of God. In every contemporary society, Christians may be addressed as strangers and exiles because they know that man's only hope of final salvation has come to him from a source outside of himself.

6
The People of God

"Once you were no people but now you
are God's people." 1 Peter 2:10

Scripture Background: 1 Peter 2:4-10

In the Gospel narrative we are told that after Jesus had
spoken the parable of the wicked husbandmen, a parable which
was spoken against the leaders of the Jews when they were
rejecting him, he called their attention to Psalm 118:22 in which
it is said: "The stone which the builders rejected has become the
head of the corner" (Matthew 21:42, Mark 12:10, Luke 20:17).
Peter probably heard Jesus when he spoke this word of warning
to those who were rejecting him. And when Peter speaks for
the apostles when they have been called before these same leaders,
he gives his witness to the resurrection and says that Jesus
"is the stone which was rejected by you builders which has
become the head of the corner." He goes on to give his witness
to Jesus as the only person through whom salvation can be
found (Acts 4:10-12). We need not be surprised therefore when
Peter in his letter, as he is dealing with the rejection of Jesus
by those who have refused to receive him, uses the same illustration of the rejected stone. Peter sets in sharp contrast the rejection of Jesus by men and the fact that in God's sight he was
chosen and precious as evidenced by God's resurrection of him
from the dead. Peter insists that Christ is a living stone. As we
think of the rejected stone that became the head of the corner, we
are using an illustration drawn from the pattern of architecture.
But Peter says that he is talking of a living Person who has the

power to communicate life to those who come to him in faith. He would remind us also of the relation of Christ as cornerstone to the other stones of the Christian faith. Peter believes that men are judged by the attitude which they take to Jesus Christ. To the believer he is the cornerstone, the foundation of his whole life of faith. To the unbeliever he is the stone of stumbling and the rock of offense. As Peter contemplates the mystery of unbelief he is aware of the way God uses the wrath of man to accomplish his purposes, as through the death of Christ for the sins of the world there has been wrought out a message of salvation which is being proclaimed to all mankind.

Peter describes the new community which has been brought into being by the proclamation of the gospel as those who are living stones, i.e. living persons who are being built into "a spiritual house, to be a holy priesthood, to offer spiritual sacrifices acceptable to God through Jesus Christ" (1 Peter 2:5). He describes the new community as he says: "You are a chosen race, a royal priesthood, a holy nation, God's own people, that you may declare the wonderful deeds of him who called you out of darkness into his marvelous light. Once you were no people but now you are God's people; once you had not received mercy but now you have received mercy" (1 Peter 2:9-10).

As we normally think of the emergence of a people in the life of the world, we will realize that there are communities based on blood such as families, or tribes, or racial groups. There are communities based primarily on geography as the people of a particular area, especially if they are under the same government, feel a deep-seated sense of unity. There are communities based on leadership, as a people receive from some outstanding leader what they conceive to be a true understanding of their human existence. We can think in this connection of the influence of leaders such as George Washington or Thomas Jefferson or in a world that is closer to us of Woodrow Wilson or Franklin D. Roosevelt or Winston Churchill, or in a somewhat different pattern of Karl Marx or Lenin or Mao or of Adolph Hitler. If the people of an area or nation have a common faith it gives them a sense of being a people. There have been many attempts to bind upon a people a common religious faith.

Peter tells us that the people whom he refers to as God's own people were formerly not a people, but that they have become a people as they have accepted the call of God in Christ. Their purpose as a people is to declare the wonderful works of him who called them from darkness into light.

They are a people who have been drawn from the whole pattern of ancient society. They cross the lines of male and female to found a community in which women are received with respect and dignity. The community crosses the lines of master and slave. A considerable portion of those to whom Peter is writing are slaves who must work for their masters according to the flesh. They are a community which crosses the lines of class and culture. Within this community there are to be found Greeks and Romans, Jews and Gentiles. Membership in the community is open to those whom the Greeks call barbarians and even to the Scythians whom the people of Peter's world thought of as the lowest of the barbarians.

The Roman Empire in which Peter lived was made up of people from many racial and cultural backgrounds. These people worshipped many different gods. The Romans would not have objected to the receiving of a new god into the pantheon even if this god was to them the most unlikely prospect, a crucified Jew. But the Christians were not willing to accept this kind of a place in the pantheon for the one whom they regarded as Lord and Saviour. They insisted that the one whom they worshipped was the true and the living God who had disclosed himself to them. All other gods were to be thought of as false gods who had no real existence.

The Romans in the beginning did not know what to think of the emergence of this new community within the context of the Roman Empire. At first they thought of Christianity as a form of Judaism. As Judaism was a permitted religion, the Christians would be accepted in the same pattern. As large numbers of those who were not of Jewish background identified themselves with the new faith, the Romans had to revise their estimate of Christianity. But they would not have objected to a new community provided that those who belonged to this community would accept a pattern of emperor worship which symbolized the unity of the various cultures of the empire in a common worship of the emperor. The Christians did not give up their normal responsibilities in the life of the empire. They continued as slave and workmen. They were prepared, in particular, to honor the emperor. They could respect the office even if they could not respect all who held it. Nero was emperor at the time that Peter wrote.

But there was one thing that the Christians could not and would not do. They could not worship the emperor because they had given their loyalty to a Person whom they believed to have a name that was above every name and that unto Him every knee should bow and that every tongue should proclaim him as Lord (Phil. 2:9-10). The Neronian persecutions which Peter was soon to face were the persecutions of an evil man who sought to put on the Christians the blame for the burning of the city of Rome. But many of the Roman emperors who sought to use the power of the empire to destroy the Christian community of faith did so because they felt that the empire could not tolerate a rapidly growing community which gave to Jesus Christ a loyalty that went beyond the loyalty they could give to the emperor of Rome.

This clash between the community of faith with its ultimate loyalty in Jesus Christ with a state which seeks to deify itself has become a crucial issue in the modern world. It was present in the effort to state German Christianity in a pattern that did not cut across the claims of Adolph Hitler. The Barmen Declaration was produced by the Confessional Church of Germany to make clear the things that people could not believe if they also believed in Jesus Christ as Lord and Saviour. This is the heart of the conflict between the various Marxist states and those who acknowledge Jesus Christ as Lord. And the community of God's people must also stand firmly against the extreme nationalism of many of the emerging states which are seeking to find their proper place in the life of the modern world, just as it must speak against any system which compulsively aligns people to any one outlook or community.

7
The Christian Way of Life

"The eyes of the Lord are upon the
righteous... The face of the Lord is
against those that do evil." 1 Peter 3:12

Scripture Background: 1 Peter 1:22; 2:1,
11, 12, 15; 3:8-12; 4:3-6

Christian conduct roots in Christian theology. The opening
part of Peter's letter is centered in his testimony to Jesus Christ.
But in the letter as a whole it is necessary to consider the implications for Christian living that are involved in the things he
is telling his readers concerning what God has done for them in
Jesus Christ. Peter's teaching concerning the pattern of Christian
living that is involved in Christian discipleship is scattered through
his letter. We have indicated in the Scripture background some
of the more significant passages. The reader will find that Peter
repeats in somewhat different settings his emphasis on love and
humility.

Our pattern of treatment will be to look first on the negative
side, i.e. on the things that Christians must not do if they are
to be faithful in their Christian discipleship. In the first verse
of the second chapter Peter says: "So put away all malice and
all guile and insincerity and envy and all slander." The things
mentioned here are essentially sins of the spirit. The calling of
attention to the sin of guile is related to his statement that no
guile was ever found on the lips of Jesus (1 Peter 2:22). The
call for the putting away of all insincerity and all slander fits
into the same pattern. Peter is asking Christians to follow the
example of Jesus in speaking the truth and being free of all
envy.

Peter strikes a different note when he writes in 2:11, "Beloved, I beseech you as aliens and exiles to abstain from the passions of the flesh that wage war against your soul." Peter is making a distinction between the sins of the spirit and the passions of the flesh that may war against the soul. This does not mean that all bodily passions are evil. All men know the meaning of hunger and thirst. Sexual desire is not in itself evil. It can, if exercised in its purity, underwrite the life of man and woman in the home. But we must realize that there can be passions of the body that war against the soul. We can think in this connection of the use of drugs in the modern world. A drug has in itself no moral quality. It may under the direction of a competent doctor be used in a ministry of healing. But we are all aware of the extent to which the wrong use of drugs lies behind moral breakdown and much of the crime of our world today. Some use of alcohol is not always wrong. But the use of alcohol may become a habit which leads to drunkenness and moves on to a slavery in which a person becomes an alcoholic and his spiritual life is threatened. There is a proper place for sex in human life. Peter himself was married and Paul is witness to the fact that Peter at times took his wife with him on trips (1 Cor. 9:5). But there is a difference between love and lust, and the sins of lust can effectively war against the soul.

In chapter 4, verses 3-6, Peter gives a vivid picture of the moral breakdown of the Gentile world in his time. He writes to his readers: "Let the time that is past suffice for doing what the Gentiles like to do, living in licentiousness, passions, drunkenness, revels, carousing, and lawless idolatry. They are surprised that you do not now join them in the same wild profligacy, and they abuse you; but they will give account to him who is ready to judge the living and the dead."

As we consider this passage we should realize that the profligacy which Peter describes was not true of all non-Christians. There were to be found among the Gentiles of the Graeco-Roman world many noble men and women. This would be particularly true of the Stoics who exalted the pursuit of virtue.

But no one who knows the life of the Gentile world of the first century would deny that Peter has given an accurate description of the way of life of many of those who lived in it. This passage from First Peter is supported by Paul's description of the world he knew as found in Romans 1:18-32. And more important for our purposes, we should realize that Peter's description of the life of his world apart from the Christian community could be accepted as an accurate description of the moral breakdown of much of our contemporary world. Peter is clear that for the Christians the things he is describing here must be a way of life with which they have made a complete break. But Peter goes on the speak a word to the profligates. He reminds them that they will give an account to him who is ready to judge the living and the dead. The reference is probably to the Christ as the judge of the living and the dead. This would be supported by Paul's statement, "We must all appear before the judgment seat of Christ, so that each one may receive good or evil, according to what he has done in the body (2 Cor. 5:10). Peter is probably thinking of Christ's judgment of all men in the context of their earthly life and also of the Judgment that comes at death. He writes in his letter, "The face of the Lord is against those that do evil" (1 Peter 3:12).

But the pattern of Christian living that Peter sets forth in his letter is not merely a matter of the sins of the spirit that we put off or the sinful passions of the flesh that war against the soul from which they must abstain. There are things that you do not do if you are a Christian. Let there be no mistake about that. But there is a positive side to the Christian way of life. In the first chapter Peter writes: "Having purified your souls by your obedience to the truth for a sincere love of the brethren, love one another earnestly from the heart" (verse 22). By his reference to the truth in this setting, Peter is thinking of the true knowledge of God and the way of life which he demands of us that comes to us through God's disclosure of himself in Christ. Peter says that the Christians will purify their souls by obedience to the truth. The call here is to purity and obedience. The

Christian virtue that is mentioned is love of the brethren. The emphasis on love of the brethren runs through the letter as a whole and is frequently repeated. For example, we read in 1 Peter 3:8: "Finally, all of you, have unity of spirit, sympathy, love of the brethren, a tender heart and a humble mind." The emphasis on Christian humility is another theme of the letter. In the ninth verse we read: "Do not return evil for evil or reviling for reviling; but on the contrary bless, for to this you have been called, that you may obtain a blessing." It is clear from this verse that Peter fully followed the teachings of Jesus in the Sermon on the Mount concerning love of enemies. Peter follows the ninth verse in a passage based on the 34th Psalm, verses 12-16, in which he affirms again freedom from guile as a mark of the way of righteousness both in the Old Testament and the New. He continues by saying: "The eyes of the Lord are upon the righteous, and his ears are open to their prayer" (verse 12).

Peter introduces a new conception in his emphasis on the Christian way of life when he calls the attention of his readers to the consideration of the impact of their way of life on those who are not Christians. He writes: "Maintain good conduct among the Gentiles, so that in case they speak against you as wrong-doers, they may see your good deeds and glorify God in the day of visitation" (1 Peter 2:12). He returns to this theme when he writes: "It is God's will that by doing right you should put to silence the ignorance of foolish men" (1 Peter 2:15). And in another setting he writes: "Keep your conscience clear, so that, when you are abused, those who revile your good behavior in Christ may be put to shame" (1 Peter 3:16).

We face here an important consideration in the effort of Christians to make converts to the Christian faith of those who were not Christians. The Christians were to be prepared to give a reason for the faith that was in them (1 Peter 3:15). But Peter knew that the strongest support for the witness to the Christian faith was the bringing into being of a community of those who lived as Christians were expected to live. This has a negative and a positive impact on the spread of the Christian faith. When those who are not Christians know that Christians profess a creed which they make little effort to follow, they can be turned against a creed which is not translated into the actual decisions of life. But when the world can witness a new community in which those who are identified with it live by obedience to the truth, speak the truth and walk in love, it can be true that the blood of the martyrs becomes the seed of the church.

8

The Christian in the State

"Honor all men. Love the brotherhood.
Fear God. Honor the emperor." 1 Peter 2:17

Scripture Background: 1 Peter 2:13-17

The opening statement of our background of Scripture reads: "Be subject for the Lord's sake to every human institution." It is clear that while Peter in this passage develops the concept of being subject for the Lord's sake to every human institution with regard to the place of the Christian in the state, he intends to let this idea cover other institutions which he will mention such as the institution of slavery and the institution of marriage. When he speaks of subjection for the Lord's sake, he means that Christians should assume their responsibilities in the various institutions of the society in which they live as part of their obedience to Christ. In a similar pattern, Paul tells Christians that they must be subject to rulers and pay their taxes for the sake of conscience (Romans 13:5-6). (The whole of Romans 13:1-8 should be examined carefully for Paul's statement of the life of the Christian in the state. Paul goes into greater detail but he and Peter are in essential agreement.)

There is a sense in which the passage we are considering is written in support of the structure of the state. Of course both Peter and Paul when they think of the state have as their background their life in the Roman Empire. Peter at this time in his life when he was probably in Rome would be fully aware of the tremendous significance of the Roman Empire. The Empire of Rome had been established at the point of the sword. Those who lived under it could make their criticisms of it, but Rome had established law and order and the Christian missionaries were able to move throughout the world they knew with some degree of protection by the Roman state. Paul and Silas were Roman citizens (Acts 16:37). There was much to be said for Rome in comparison with other governments in the ancient world. We can appreciate the function of Rome as we face today on a world-wide scale a breakdown of effective government in which human life is increasingly insecure.

Peter urges subjection to the emperor as supreme and to the governors as sent by him. Those to whom Peter wrote were in a part of the empire in which they would have to deal in the main with the governors who were sent by the emperor. It is in this setting that Peter says that the governors are sent by the emperor "to punish those who do wrong and to praise those who do right" (1 Peter 2:14). Peter is in agreement with Paul as he states here the basic concept of the just state in which the power of government is used to punish those who do wrong and to reward those who do right. Every effective state must have a police force to enforce obedience to the law. We must realize, of course, that police forces can be misused. Solzhenitsyn would testify to this in his experiences with the Russian police. Peter says to the Christians of Asia: "It is God's will that by doing right you should put to silence the ignorance of foolish men" (1 Peter 2:15). This is another example of the call to Christians to regulate their conduct in concern for its effect on those who could be their enemies. (See also 1 Peter 2:12 and 3:16.)

The Christians are to live as free men but are not to use their freedom as a pretext for evil. There is a difference between liberty and license.

In saying that Christians live in freedom, Peter does not mean they are to use their liberty to do as they please. They will experience true freedom when they live as servants of God. In this setting we can think of the words of Peter when he and John were called before the rulers of the Jews following his speech after healing in the name of Jesus a man who had been lame from his birth. The rulers of the Jews "charged them not to speak or teach at all in the name of Jesus" (Acts 4:18). Peter as the spokesman for the two apostles answered them, "Whether it is right in the sight of God to listen to you rather than to God, you must judge; for we cannot but speak of what we have seen and heard" (Acts 4:19-20). We must realize that Peter and John are dealing with the leaders of the Jews, but the principle is the same when the community of faith is confronted by the power of a secular state. The community of God's people cannot surrender its right to propagate its faith, i.e. to "declare the wonderful deeds of him who has called you out of darkness into his wonderful light" (1 Peter 2:9). These words of Peter were frequently quoted as the leaders of the Confessional Church in Germany refused to keep silence or to distort the message which had been committed to them to suit the pattern of German Christianity demanded by Adolph Hitler.

Peter says that Christians must "Honor all men." In commenting on this clause Selwyn writes: "St. Peter lays down the obligation of the respect and courtesy due to human personality as such, an obligation which is inconsistent in the political sphere with those principles of absolute or totalitarian government which sacrifice the individual wholly to the State, and in the economic sphere with all systems and methods which regard men simply as 'hands' " (*The First Epistle of Peter*, p. 174).

Over against his urging of Christians to be obedient to the demands of the state within the limits that are possible to them as Christians, Peter slips in the injunction, "Love the brotherhood." Here the community of God's people is contrasted with the community of the state based on authority supported by military power. Peter describes the community of faith as a people who are held together by their love of each other. The community of love is first of all a community of those who have responded to the love of the Christ for them as it has been witnessed to in Christian preaching. But the one whom they have acknowledged as Lord and Saviour has said to them: "A new commandment I give to you, that you love one another; even as I have loved you, that you also love one another. By this all men will know that you are my disciples, if you have love for one another" (John 13:34-35). Napoleon is reported to have said when he was in exile that he and Caesar and Alexander had built their kingdoms on force and that they had crumbled into dust, but that Jesus built his kingdom on love and that there were millions who were living now who would die for him.

Peter also writes to his readers, "Fear God." It was said of John Knox that he feared God and that because he feared God he feared not the face of man. We are told in Proverbs 9:10 that "the fear of the Lord is the beginning of wisdom." As we seek to strike at the roots of the moral breakdown in our society as reflected in the rising rate of crime, we need to remember that there is no substitute for the fear of God. While love for God is primary in faith, it is naïve to believe that love and "fear" are mutually exclusive. When we seek to keep the commandments of God because we know that his commandments are the expression of his righteous will for us, we express love, respect, awe, loyalty, trust, praise and "fear." Faith is a more complex and balanced act than either love or fear would be without the rich response of personality that includes both love and fear as well as other dimensions of emotional experience. The important and unique aspect of the Christian faith, however, is the conviction that all of our attitudes are subject to God's renewing grace. Both love and fear are transformed. They become new and healthy. Thus, in confidence and gratitude, we can listen humbly to the words of Paul in Galatians: "Do not be deceived; God is not mocked, for whatever a man sows, that he will also reap" (Galatians 6:7).

Peter's closing injunction is "Honor the emperor." He is urging that Christians contribute to the order and stability of society by respecting the head of the state. They should honor office and the one who serves in it if he deserving of respect.

But there is a difference between honoring the emperor and worshipping the emperor. Worship belongs to God alone. Christians could not worship the emperor because in so doing they would have denied their basic conviction that Jesus Christ is Lord.

Even as Peter writes the lines are being drawn for the great conflict which will last for centuries, in which the power of the Roman state will be used to destroy a community which is based on faith and love. The profession of the Christian faith was to be branded as a crime to be punished by death. Rome was to be thought of as the great enemy of God's people. Some of the persecutors were to be evil men such as Nero. Others were to be statesmen who were seeking to bring unity to the state. But the Roman Empire was to fail to destroy the Christian church. Constantine came to power in time to make the Christian faith the official religion of the Roman state. And the message of the gospel was to be carried from Rome to the ends of the earth. The Rome of Caesar was to become the Rome of Peter.

9
The Christian
in the Economic Order

"If when you do right and suffer for it you
take it patiently, you have God's approval." 1 Peter 2:20

Scripture Background: 1 Peter 2:18-20

Peter needed to speak a word to the slaves who were members of the Christian communities in the churches of Asia to
whom his letter was addressed. The message of the gospel was
proclaimed without respect of persons to all who would hear it.
Slavery was an accepted pattern of life in the Roman Empire,
and we can therefore be sure that a considerable number of
those who would hear Peter's letter when it was read in the
churches of Asia would be slaves. Slavery in the Roman Empire
was not set up on a racial basis. Men were sold into slavery
for debts they could not pay. And many of those who were
slaves had been sold as captives of war. In some cases the
slave might actually have a richer cultural background than that
of his master. But slavery in the Roman Empire had in it the
possibilities of great cruelty. And the slave revolt under Spartacus
which at one time controlled much of southern Italy lay in the
not too distant future.

Even in the brief references to slavery in Peter's letter there
are some things said which do not make pleasant reading. There
are masters who are kind and gentle, but there are others who
are overbearing. As a pattern of enforcing obedience among
slaves, beatings were given to slaves. In some cases these were
administered because the slaves had done wrong. But in other

cases slaves were beaten even when it was clear the they had done what was right.

As we think about the institution of slavery in the ancient world and also in the life of America in times which are not so distant from us, we are apt to rebel violently against it. We do not like to think of an institution in which one person owns another. We do not like to think of a slave market in which human beings are sold to the highest bidder. These things violate that respect of persons as individuals which is involved in Peter's injunction, "Honor all men" (1 Peter 2:17). We can respect those who felt that they were acting as Christians when they sought to eliminate slavery. While the pattern of slavery which was known in the ancient world may continue in some isolated areas, we can rejoice that this particular form of the economic order has been eliminated in most civilized nations.

But Peter had to face the reality of the situation which actually existed in the world in which he lived. Neither he nor the slaves could alter the basic economic structure of the society they knew. As we consider Peter's treatment of slavery, we should also be familiar with Paul's discussion of it in Colossians 3:20—4:1 and in Ephesians 6:5-9, and also the letter to Philemon. These treatments are given in greater detail than in Peter's letter and they also include the word to the owners of slaves. Peter speaks his message to slaves against the background of his basic injunction to Christians to be subject for the Lord's sake to every human institution (1 Peter 2:13). He urges the slaves to be submissive to their masters with all respect, not only to the kind and gentle but also to the overbearing. He fully realizes that this will mean for some slaves suffering which they do not feel they deserve. But he sets their suffering in the light of their relation to God in Christ when he says to them: "one is approved, if, mindful of God, he endures pain while suffering unjustly" (1 Peter 2:19). He repeats this idea when he says: "When you do right and suffer for it, you have God's approval." And then Peter tells them that the bearing of undeserved suffering is part of their calling as they are followers of the Christ who has given us the best example that we have of a person who suffers unjustly. In this way Peter has moved into the basic theme of his letter, which is to prepare the Christians of Asia for times of testing which he is certain they will face as part of their entering into the fellowship of the sufferings of Christ. But this will be the theme of another chapter.

We should realize that Christianity in the ancient world, while it was forced to tolerate the institution of slavery and encourage slaves to submit to their masters, did do much to soften the inevitable abuses of slavery. The very fact that slaves and owners found themselves in the fellowship of the Christian church in which they recognized each other as brothers must have had a profound impact on the conditions of slaves. Paul's letter to Philemon is a little gem of a letter which witnesses to this process. The letter to the Colossians who were owners of slaves includes the admonition: "Masters, treat your slaves justly and fairly, knowing that you also have a Master in heaven" (Colossians 4:1). And Ephesians adds: "and that there is no partiality with him" (6:9).

We live today in an economic order in which slavery as it was known in the ancient world and for many years in the life of America has been banished. But we need to take a close look at the capitalistic society of our contemporary world. This pattern of the economic order has grown out of the industrial revolution in which the capacity of man to produce for his needs and wants has been enormously increased. We live in a world in which much of the work that used to be done by slaves is done much more efficiently by power machines. We live in a world which has been able to achieve for many of its people a much higher standard of living for the masses of its people than that which was known before the days of the Industrial Revolution. We live in a world in which much of the work of the industrial order is controlled by great companies that in some cases are owned by millions of stockholders. It is a world in which Christians who are in positions of power are free to work for the improved structure of their society to meet the needs of all their people. In the early days of the industrial society, workers faced difficult conditions and inadequate compensation for long hours of work.

There is much to be said for our contemporary society, but no one would deny that a modern industrial society has its problems. There is often major unemployment and many people are forced to give the labor of their lives to tasks that are dull and uninteresting. In this kind of society there may be many workers who need to hear Peter's word to the slaves of the ancient world. In this he tells them to accept the life situation which they face as those who are mindful of the God who has set them in it and as those who seek to perform their daily tasks in a way which will merit his approval.

We face a different situation when we look out on the world of Marxism. We need to remember that Karl Marx wrote his *Capital and Labor* in protest against the abuses which he saw in the industrial order in its initial impact on the life of man. Much of the material for his book is taken from the reports of English supervisors who made written records of the conditions which they found in surveying the industrial life of their nation. Marx does not seem to realize that he is facing here the beginnings of a pattern of social control that was to profoundly modify the capitalism he knew. But the growth of Marxism in the period since it was introduced in Russia during the First World War is amazing. The thought of Marx and of those who followed him dominates the life of much of eastern Europe, of Russia and Siberia, and China and much of Southeast Asia. And we are bound to be aware of many things that have happened, particularly in China, which have struck at deep rooted evils. But we need also to be aware of the freedom that have been lost in Marxist lands by the great masses of mankind. Solzhenitsyn in *The Gulag Archipelago* makes us keenly aware of a pattern of slavery that has been imposed on millions of human beings. If we compare it to the slavery which Peter knew in the Roman Empire, we will probably reach the conclusion that the slavery that was found in the Graeco-Roman world was less damaging to that respect for human personality that should be part of the Christian faith. In this setting the words of Peter to Christians who were forced to live as slaves in the Roman Empire may have some relevancy to Christians who are trying to live in obedience to the Lord Jesus Christ in Marxist lands.

10

The Christian
in the
Institution of Marriage

"You are joint heirs of the grace of life."
1 Peter 3:7

Scripture Background: 1 Peter 3:1-7

Peter applies the principle, "Be subject for the Lord's sake, to every human institution," to the life of the Christian in the institution of marriage. Paul describes the institution of marriage as he writes: "A married woman is bound by law to her husband as long as he lives; but if her husband dies she is discharged from the law concerning the husband. Accordingly, she will be called an adulteress if she lives with another man while her husband is alive. But if her husband dies she is free from that law, and if she marries another man she is not an adulteress" (Romans 7:2-3). We should understand that Paul in this passage from Romans is not talking primarily about marriage. He is using the understanding of marriage which he sets forth to illustrate the way in which the death of Christ, if accepted by the believer, sets that person free from the law of sin and death. But the incidental nature of this reference to marriage does not alter the fact that it is based on his understanding of the institution. Peter is contrast to Paul was a married man. But the probability is that Peter would have shared the understanding of the institution of marriage which Paul gives us. The statement of Paul is that the self-giving of one man and one woman to each other in marriage creates a relationship which is expected to last until it is terminated by death. This idea has been written into the marriage vows in the phrase "until

death us shall part." The Christian church must not surrender
the concept of the finality of marriage to suit the changing
patterns of a secular society. When we say this we must realize
that we must face the actual situations of life with a degree
of realism. Paul does this when he faces the situation when
the unbelieving partner who is not a Christian does not desire
to continue the marriage relationship with a partner who has
become a Christian. Paul writes: "In such a case the brother
or sister is not bound" (1 Cor. 7:15). In this setting he adds
the sentence: "For God has called us to peace."

In his treatment of the Christian in the institution of marriage
Peter emphasizes the submission of wives to their husbands.
We should realize that there is in Christianity an understanding
of the equality of man and woman in Christ. Paul writes: "As
many of you as were baptized into Christ have put on Christ.
There is neither Jew nor Greek, there is neither slave nor free,
there is neither male nor female; for you are all one in Christ
Jesus" (Galatians 3:27-28). It is in harmony with this understanding of a unity in Christ which transcends even the ineradica-
ble distinction of male and female that woman is treated as a
person of dignity and responsibility in the Pauline world church.
But Paul goes far beyond Peter in the limitations that he puts
on women in situations that are more or less local and tem-
porary. We must remember that Peter was writing to readers
who lived in a situation in which the liberation of woman as
we know it today had not been thought of. If Peter were writing
today he would probably express himself somewhat differently.
We are probably true to the thought of Peter when we say
that marriage is an institution in which both husbands and
wives need to assume the obligations involved in a pattern of
being mutually subject to each other for the Lord's sake. In
giving his advice to husbands, Peter says: "Likewise you husbands,
live considerately with your wives, bestowing honor on the woman
as the weaker sex" (1 Peter 3:7). In speaking of the woman
as the weaker sex Peter may not be doing more than referring
to the fact that probably in most marriages men have greater

physical strength than women. This does not settle the question as to the comparative creativity of men and women. And many women have been able to excel in athletics. In the actual combat of war and in very strenuous physical labor men have usually been given a special responsibility.

As part of his advice concerning marriage Peter makes an interesting reference to the beauty of women. He writes to the wives: "Let not yours be the outward adorning with braiding of hair, decoration of gold, and wearing of robes, but let it be the hidden person of the heart with the imperishable jewel of a gentle and quiet spirit, which in God's sight is very precious" (1 Peter 3:3-4). Certainly as we think of life in the modern world, women within the limits of their resources should seek to make themselves attractive in appearance. Peter would probably not have objected to this. But the important thing to think of is the inner beauty of the spirit. This would apply to both men and women. Even if a person has an attractive figure and wears expensive clothes we can come to feel adversely toward that person if he or she consistently reveals a cruel and lustful and arrogant spirit. And even if a person has a physical appearance that leaves something to be desired and is dressed in inexpensive clothing, we feel the radiance of love and purity and genuine humility. Peter has related this whole matter to our attitude to God when he says that the imperishable jewel of a gentle and quiet spirit is in God's sight very precious. It can also be attractive to others. Chrysostom is reported to have said that the pagan philosophers said to him that the most attractive thing about the Christians was the quality of the women who were to be found among them. And if we are thinking of relating the simple things of life to God, we can express Peter's word to slaves in the context of the home. In a situation which may sometimes seem to be tense limiting, and unfair, as a husband or a wife we can still seek to do what is right. Even if we are constantly subjected to criticism we have God's approval if we take it patiently.

Peter tells husbands and wives that they must live together

as "joint heirs of the grace of life" (1 Peter 3:7). Scholars are generally agreed that by the expression, "the grace of life," Peter means eternal life. For example, Bigg says that the phrase grace of life "is rightly understood by Alford to mean God's gracious gift of life eternal" (*St. Peter and St. Jude*, p. 155). And Peter himself defines the phrase as he says in 1:13, "Set your hope fully upon the grace that is coming to you at the revelation of Jesus Christ."

What does it mean when Christian husbands and wives are told to live together in this world as those who are heirs together of eternal life? Marriage is both a human and a divine institution. It is deeply rooted in the life of earth, and those who become a part of the resurrection world of God which lies beyond death go into a world in which they neither marry or are given in marriage (Luke 20:35). But this does not mean that in that world they will not know each other and know that in the life of earth they have lived in the intimacy of marriage. Paul has told us that love, faith, and hope are among the things that abide the passing from this world to the resurrection world of God. He has told us also that in that world we shall know even as we are known (1 Cor. 13:12-13). And if we know even as we are known, husbands and wives will know each other and will know also the children that have come into existence through the element of creativity that is in marriage. It will mean also that these children will know that they have come into being in this way. It is this knowledge that passes into the life of eternity that sets man, woman, and child in a trinity of being that cannot be altered. What should be the marks of the kind of life that a husband and wife should live together if they seek to live together as those who are joint heirs of eternal life? We are true to the thinking of Peter if we mention three marks of Christian living which he consistently emphasizes. The first is love—love of each other, love of the brotherhood, and love of those who could be our enemies. The second is freedom from guile, the living together of a life of sincerity and speaking the truth. The third is humility, the readiness to walk humbly before God and to wait for his divine lifting up. Peter says husbands and wives should live together as heirs together of eternal life in order that their prayers may not be hindered. Bigg comments: "The two cannot join in prayer, as they ought to do, for a blessing on their married life, if there is injustice between them" (*St. Peter and St. Jude,* p. 154). It is also true that if Christian husbands and wives live together so that they can pray together, they can be expected to stay together.

11

The Suffering and Death
of Jesus Christ

"He himself bore our sins in his body on
the tree." 1 Peter 2:24

Scripture Background: 1 Peter 2:21-25

This passage on the suffering and death of Jesus Christ is
one of the most important passages in Peter's letter to the Christians in the provinces of Asia. Peter moves into it almost inci-
dentally as he is speaking his word to the slaves. He has told the
slaves that if when they do right and suffer for it patiently,
they have God's approval. From this example of bearing patiently
suffering that is not deserved, his mind moves at once to what
for him is the great example of undeserved suffering, the suffering of the Christ on the cross.

As he does this he also becomes involved in the basic theme
of his letter as a whole. He is writing to the Christians of Asia
to prepare them for the experiences of undeserved suffering which
he expects them to have in the near future, and he seeks to help
them understand their sufferings as part of their call to know
Jesus in their fellowship with his sufferings.

The passage before us has been traditionally considered by
many scholars as a description and interpretation of the sufferings of the Christ by one who was an eyewitness of the event he
was writing about. In 1 Peter 5:1 Peter writes: "I exhort you...
as a witness of the sufferings of Christ." We do not know the
movements of Peter after the time of his denial when Jesus turned
and looked upon Peter when he was being taken from the exam-
ination by Annas to the trial before Caiaphas. We do know that

John was present at the crucifixion. We have nothing to prove that Peter could not have been. And if the basic content of this letter reflects the thought of Peter or, as we feel, was even suggested by him, we have his own statement that he was a witness to the last days of Jesus and perhaps even to the crucifixion.

The passage before us does read as the writing of a person who has been an eyewitness. Selwyn says that Peter emphasizes the meekness of Christ. He goes on to say: "And he writes about it as one who had himself witnessed it" (*The First Epistle of Peter*, p. 91). He continues: "St. Paul has nothing corresponding to those intimate touches of detail with which St. Peter describes Him [Jesus]... Nor is anything similar found in any other Epistle." If we do have here in a written document an authentic description of the sufferings of Christ by an eyewitness we have a passage of great significance.

Peter writes to his readers: "Christ also suffered for you, leaving you an example, that you should follow in his steps" (1 Peter 2:21). The way in which the Christ bore his suffering has set for his disciples an example that they should follow. We can imitate the Christ as he sets an example for us. We cannot imitate him in many of the mighty works which appear in the gospel traditions, such as the feeding of the five thousand, because we have not been trusted with this power. But we can imitate him in most of the things Peter mentions.

We must think of the sufferings of Jesus as going much deeper than the setting of an example. There had to be an inner necessity in the sufferings of Jesus. Jesus said to Peter at the time of the arrest: "Put your sword into its sheath; shall I not drink the cup which the Father has given me?" (John 18:11). His prayer in Gethsemane shows the same sense of necessity. And as the risen Lord he tells Cleopas that it was necessary that the Christ should suffer these things and enter into his glory (Luke 24:26).

Peter tells the Christians of the churches of Asia that Christ suffered for them. In doing this he sets the pattern of asking each

individual Christian to realize that the sufferings of the Christ were
for him. This would apply to Christians today as well as to the
Christians of Asia in the first century. He does not in this statement explain the way in which the sufferings of Christ were for
them. But the answer to this question comes out as he continues
his testimony. In the opening words of verse 22, Peter says of
Jesus: "He committed no sin." In this he affirms the sinlessness
of Jesus. We cannot completely imitate him in this for, to some
extent, we sin daily in thought, word, and deed. We must realize
that not all of the contemporaries of Jesus considered him sinless
when they judged him by their standards. There were some who
branded him as "a glutton and a drunkard, a friend of tax
collectors and sinners" (Matthew 11:19).

But the very charges made against Jesus turn out to his
advantage when seen in their proper perspective. We cannot
consider him wrong when he acted as a friend of sinners. The
emphasis on his sinlessness is important to establish the fact that
it was not for his own sins that he suffered and died. Peter goes
on to say that "no guile was found on his lips." This means
that he always spoke the truth, and, consequently, that freedom
from guile should be a mark of those who are followers of Jesus.
And he lived up to his own teachings when Peter can write:
"When he was reviled he did not revile in return." He could
be fearless in condemning hypocrisy as in his indictment of the
way of life of the scribes and Pharisees that are mentioned in
Matthew 23 and in other places. When he suffered he was aware
of the judgment that might in the justice of God come on those
who were causing him to suffer, but he did not threaten them.
Instead he trusted himself to him who judges justly. In all of
these marks of the suffering Christ which Peter mentions in verses
22 and 23, with the exception of the reference to his sinlessness,
there is set forth a way of life which his followers can seek to
imitate.

In verse 24 Peter says of Jesus: "He himself bore our sins
in his body on the tree." Selwyn quotes from Archbishop Leighton
the statement: "The sins of all, in all ages before and after, who

were to be saved, all their guiltiness met together on his back upon the Cross" (*The First Epistle of Peter*, p. 97). And in the same verse Peter himself gives his statement of the purpose of the death of Jesus when he says that Jesus died "that we might die to sin and live to righteousness." This was, according to Peter, also the basic purpose of the Father in the sending of his Son.

In the closing part of verse 24, Peter writes: "By his wounds you have been healed." This is a quotation from the description of the suffering servant in the 53rd chapter of Isaiah (see verse 5). In using this quotation, Peter demonstrates the pattern of the gospel tradition in which Jesus confesses that he is the Messiah but adopts for himself the concept of a Messiah who must accomplish his work through his suffering and death. This framework also lies behind the reference in 1:11 to the prediction of the sufferings of the Christ found in the prophets.

The great passages on the sufferings and death of the Christ which are found throughout the Scriptures usually end with a passage in which the witness to the resurrection is given as God's vindication of the suffering servant in the world that lies beyond death. Peter does not do this in the passage we are considering. But the idea is involved as Peter tells his readers that they were once straying like sheep but that they have now returned to the one who is the Shepherd and Guardian of their souls. It is indeed interesting to note that the picture of Peter given in Acts is compatible with this positive witness. In his sermon at Pentecost, Peter makes it clear that he is talking of Jesus of Nazareth and says: "This Jesus, delivered up according to the definite plan and foreknowledge of God, you crucified and killed by the hands of lawless men. But God raised him up, having loosed the pangs of death, because it was not possible for him to be held by it" (Acts 2:23-24).

And the letter of Peter is remarkable for the way in which Peter consistently combines both for Jesus and for his followers the concept of suffering with the concept of the glory that is to follow. The prophets predict "the sufferings of Christ and the subsequent glory" (1 Peter 1:11). And in 1 Peter 1:21 he writes:

"Through him [Jesus] you have confidence in God, who raised him from the dead and gave him glory, so that your faith and hope are in God." In the passage in which Peter affirms that he is a witness of the sufferings of Christ, he also says that he is "a partaker in the glory that is to be revealed" (5:1). And in the passage in which he is bringing his letter to a close he reminds his readers for whom he has predicted an experience of suffering that "the same experience of suffering is required of your brotherhood throughout the world." He continues: "And after you have suffered a little while, the God of all grace, who has called you to his eternal glory in Christ, will himself restore, establish, and strengthen you" (1 Peter 5:10).

12

Prepared to Make a Defense
. . . for the Hope That Is in You

Scripture Background: 1 Peter 3:13-18

Peter's call to the Christians of Asia to be always prepared to make a defense of the hope that is in them is found in a somewhat rambling passage in which Peter repeats, in a slightly altered form, some of the things he has already said. We have also the distinction between those who suffer for wrong doing and those who suffer for the sake of righteousness. And he passes again from the thought of those who find that it is God's will for them to suffer for righteousness to another statement about the death of Christ which needs to be added to the statements considered in chapter 11. He says: "Christ also died for sins once for all, the righteous for the unrighteous, that he might bring us to God" (1 Peter 3:18). In his expression "once for all" he emphasizes the fact that Christ's sacrifice had to be made but that once it has been made it will never need to be repeated.

But the verse which centers our interest in this chapter is 1 Peter 3:15, which reads: "But in your hearts reverence Christ as Lord. Always be prepared to make a defense to any one who calls you to account for the hope that is in you, yet do it with gentleness and reverence." When Peter reminds his readers of the hope that is in them, he is thinking of their hope of eternal salvation. He has defined this hope in the beginning of his letter where he tells his readers that they have been born anew to a living hope through the resurrection of Jesus Christ from the

dead "to an inheritance which is imperishable, undefiled, and unfading, kept in heaven for you, who by God's power are guard-
ed through faith for a salvation ready to be revealed in the last
time." (See chapter 1 for a fuller discussion of this.)

When Peter tells his readers that they must be always prepared to make a defense to anyone who calls them to account
for the hope that is in them, he is giving them advice that is
supported by the portrait of his own witness in the book of Acts.
This narrative of Christians in the first century shows few if any
who had given a more effective account of the hope that was
in them than Simon Peter. In Acts his whole life as the leader
and spokesman for the apostles is devoted to giving his Christian
testimony. In addition, Acts points to three crucial experiences in
Peter's life when his testimony was given with courage and integrity. The first of these was his statement to the Jerusalem mob
after the coming of the Holy Spirit at Pentecost. The second was
his message to the leaders of the Jews when he and John were
called before them following the healing of the man who had been
a cripple from birth. The third was his speech to the Gentiles
assembled in the home of Cornelius, the Roman centurion at
Caesarea. It was this speech that opened the way for the reception of Gentiles into the Christian church.

While these accounts vary greatly in their settings and in the
details of the story that is told, they have in them certain elements that are common to all of them. In each of these stories
the starting point is something which has happened which demands
explanation. In the Pentecost story, it is the coming of the Holy
Spirit which changed the community of faith from a small group
meeting behind closed doors to a community that took to the
streets to give their testimony. In the scene before the Sanhedrin,
there is the healing of a man who had been lame from birth. In
the speech at Caesarea, there is the unusual fact that a Roman
centurion had gathered together his friends to hear a message
from Peter. While these experiences differ widely, they are all
understood as brought about by the work of the Holy Spirit.
In each of these experiences the testimony of Peter is given to

Jesus Christ as to who he is and as to what he can do for those who will receive him. In the Pentecost experience there is a major response in which Christianity is remembered as becoming almost a mass movement in Jerusalem. In the speech to the Sanhedrin we do not have the response of faith, but we do have the recognition by the members of the Sanhedrin that something has happened which cannot be explained if they reject the explanation which Peter gives. In the speech at Caesarea there is a movement of the Spirit in Peter's audience which prepared the way for his decision to administer baptism to these Gentiles and to receive them into the full fellowship of the Christian church. In the perspective of Acts it would have been difficult to listen to Peter without feeling the call to respond in love, faith, and obedience.

Peter, in his call to his readers to be prepared to make a defense to anyone who called them to account for the hope that was in them, does not make any direct reference to his own experience. He is asking his readers to be prepared to make defense of their hope of an eternal salvation to those who asked for it in their own life situations. His message can also be addressed to us in our life situation as we live in a secular world in which there are many who have given up all hope of such a salvation.

In making this "preparation," we have Peter's defense of his own faith as given in his speeches in Acts and in the letter we are studying. But we are not limited to this. We have Paul's letters, as well as Luke's account of Paul's conversion in Acts, chapter 9, verses 1-30, and of his speeches in the closing chapters of Acts. In the latter Paul defends his way of life while a prisoner. This material, as well as the Gospel and letters of John, provides examples of creative witness which help us. Thus inspired, Robert Browning in his poem, "A Death in a Desert," puts in the mouth of the dying John the statement: "I say, the acknowledgment of God in Christ accepted by thy reason solves for thee all questions in the earth or out of it" (*Browning's Complete Poems,* p. 390).

But those who would be prepared to make a defense of the hope that is in them are not limited to the testimony of others to Jesus. They can consider also the things that Jesus himself has said as they have been preserved for us in the four Gospels.

And many of us may also wish to turn to things more direct-ly related to our own experience. We may wish to refer to our own sense of the ring of truth as we read the New Testament witness to Jesus. We may agree with Paul when he tells the Thessalonians that the gospel came to them "not only in word, but also in power and in the Holy Spirit and with full conviction" (1 Thess. 1:5). We may also want to refer to those we have known in our own life contacts whose lives have witnessed to the reality of their faith.

It is interesting for us to call attention to the way in which Peter, after he has urged his readers to be always prepared to defend their faith, goes on to say: "Yet do it with gentleness and reverence; and keep your conscience clear." Peter follows this with the hope that they will so live that when they are abused those who revile their good behavior in Christ may be put to shame (1 Peter 3:16). Peter is thinking in terms of evangelism through the witness of the Christian life as well as evangelism through testimony.

13

The Gospel
Was Preached to the Dead

"He went and preached to the spirits in
prison." I Peter 3:19
"The gospel was preached even to the
dead." 1 Peter 4:6

Scripture Background: 1 Peter 3:18-22;
4:5-6

The first passage we are considering in this chapter is one in
which Peter moves again from his concern with the suffering of
the righteous to a further consideration of the suffering and death
of the Christ. He has said that Christ "died for sins once for
all, the righteous for the unrighteous, that he might bring us to
God." With this background he proceeds to a further discussion
of the death of Christ. He says of Christ's death "being put to
death in the flesh but made alive in the spirit; in which he went
and preached to the spirits in prison" (1 Peter 3:18-19). He defines these spirits as those, "who formerly did not obey, when
God's patience waited in the days of Noah, during the building
of the ark" (1 Peter 3:20).

Let us consider the first part of this statement. Peter says
that Jesus was put to death in the flesh but made alive in the
spirit. The element of violence is suggested here in the words
"put to death." Peter says that the body of Jesus died as a result of the treatment he received on the cross. He goes on to
say that he was made alive in the spirit. The rather obvious
meaning of this is that the spirit of Jesus survived the death
of his body. In this Peter is saying of Jesus something that may
also be true of us. We know people as embodied spirits. There
is a sense in which this the only way we know them. Human
beings communicate with each other through their bodies. But

we do not believe that the spirit perishes with the death of the
body. We have the word of Jesus that he has prepared for us a
place in his Father's house and the promise that he will come
again and take us to himself that where he is we may be also
(John 14:2-3). This is a part of the hope that is in us which
Peter refers to in 1 Peter 3:15.

But in the case of the death of Jesus, Peter tells us that his
disembodied spirit went into the realm of departed spirits and
preached to the spirits of those who were lost at the time of the
flood. We are not told anything of the content of this preaching
or anything of the response that was made to it. But we touch
here a tradition that was strong enough in the first centuries of
the history of the church to be included in one of the oldest and
most popular of the early creeds, the creed which is known to us
as The Apostles' Creed, in the words, "He descended into hell."
This creed is used in many worship services today. The word for
hell which is used here is the familiar word for the world of departed spirits. But the reference to them as those who formerly
did not obey makes it clear that Peter at least is thinking of
those who were not saved. Peter seems to assume that these
people who died at the time of Noah were still living as spirits
that could be preached to. We should notice in passing that in
the passage we are considering the mind of Peter moves from the
thought of those who were living at the time of Noah and were
disobedient to Noah's salvation through water (the water floated
the ark), and from the water of the flood to the water of baptism.
We have his statement to his readers: "Baptism . . . saves you . . . as
an appeal to God for a clear conscience, through the resurrection
of Jesus Christ." The full meaning of his statement is not clear.
It is the only reference to the sacraments in his letter and is also
a witness to the resurrection following his statement that Jesus was
made alive in the spirit. It has no bearing on the understanding of
what happened when he preached to the spirits in prison. This
statement on baptism is followed by a very significant passage in
which Peter affirms all that was involved in the ascension of
Jesus following his resurrection. Peter tells us in verse 22 that

Jesus Christ "has gone into heaven and is at the right hand of God, with angels, authorities, and powers subject to him."

There is a reference to the preaching of the gospel to the dead in the fourth chapter of 1 Peter. It comes as Peter thinks of the profilgates who abuse the Christians because they will not join them in licentious living. Peter is speaking of them as he says: "They will give account to him who is ready to judge the living and the dead" (1 Peter 4:5). It is clear that in this verse Peter considers the risen and ascended Jesus as the one who is ready to judge the living and the dead. This thought is affirmed by Paul when he says: "We must all appear before the judgment seat of Christ, so that each one may receive good or evil, according to what he has done in the body" (2 Cor. 5:10). It is against the background of his statement that Jesus is ready to judge the living and the dead that Peter writes: "For this is why the gospel was preached even to the dead, that though judged in the flesh like men, they might live in the spirit like God" (1 Peter 4:6). It is obvious that as Peter writes this he is expecting a consummation of history in the not too distant future, because he follows his reference to the gospel that was preached to the dead by the statement that "the end of all things is at hand." In this statement Peter joins Paul in his expectation of the return of Christ in the near future. We need to put beside the reference of Peter to the gospel as preached to the dead an almost incidental statement of Paul, "whether we live or whether we die, we are the Lord's. For to this end Christ died and lived again, that he might be Lord both of the dead and of the living" (Romans 14:8-9).

In looking at our biblical material, we need to consider also a statement in Ephesians in which the writer of this letter says of Christ: "When he ascended on high he led a host of captives, and he gave gifts to men. He who descended is he who also ascended far above all the heavens, that he might fill all things (Ephesians 4:8,10). We have in the thought expressed here the unity of the idea of descent into what he calls the lower parts of the earth and ascent into heaven. The two ideas are united in

Peter's thought. This writer does suggest that there was some response to Jesus when he descended to the lowest parts of the earth.

As we consider the biblical witness to the concept of Jesus making as a disembodied spirit a descent into hell and the idea of his preaching to the dead, we must realize that the biblical writers are thinking in terms of a three-storied universe with the earth at its center with heaven above the clouds and with hell as a place in the lowest depths of the earth. They used the cosmology which they had because it was shared both by them and by those to whom they were writing. We live with the knowledge of the universe we have today with the earth as a small planet in one of many solar systems. We must seek to express our basic convictions in a way that is relevant to what we know about the universe today. But the fundamental issues of the fate of those who died with faith in Christ, and those who die without knowing of him or in rejection of the knowledge they have, and the responsibility of those who must preach the gospel in the context of the world we know abide with us regardless of the cosmology we use.

In commenting on the passages we have considered Jowett writes: "Let the question be stated with perfect frankness—are the sinful who have never heard of Jesus, to pass into the darkness of a final destiny, a darkness which will never be illumined by the gospel and ministry of redemption? Here is the scriptural answer to that painful quest: 'He went and preached unto the spirits in prison' " (*The Redeemed Family of God*, p. 143).

We must realize that the biblical material with which we are dealing is too limited and too uncertain in its interpretation for us to seek to build on it any positive doctrine as an essential element of our creed. But what we can do is to realize afresh the limitations under which we operate in the context of the world in which we live. We cannot be sure that we know fully what was involved in the thought of Paul when he said that Christ died and lived again that he might be Lord both of the dead and the living (Romans 14:9). From what we know of Jesus as he revealed himself to us and as he lives among us we are happy to know that his is the Lord of the dead. (Consider in this setting John 5:25-29.)

We are thinking primarily here of Peter and we can certainly say that whatever thoughts Peter had about the preaching of the gospel to the dead did not in any way affect the urgency of his understanding of the necessity of preaching the gospel to those who are living in our contemporary world. His letter as a whole is filled with his sense of the urgency of the task of evangelism. And it was Peter who was speaking of Jesus as he said to the Sanhedrin of the Jews: "And there is salvation in no one else, for there is no other name under heaven given among men by which we must be saved" (Acts 4:12). Even if the gospel is preached to the dead it must be the good news of what God had done for man in Christ.

14

Good Stewards
of
God's Varied Grace

"As each has received a gift, employ it
for one another, as good stewards of God's
varied grace." 1 Peter 4:10

Scripture Background: 1 Peter 4:7-11

The passage of five verses which is our background of Scripture is a rather poorly organized collection of injunctions which are in themselves Christian and are important as filling out the picture of Peter's understanding of the pattern of Christian living. The passage is followed by the well known passage on the fiery trial which brings the fourth chapter to its close. We have selected the tenth verse which deals with the theme of giving a good stewardship of the particular gifts of God's grace which we have received to center our study of the passage. It is significant in its own meaning and it gives some unity to the latter part of the passage. We will give before discussing this verse a somewhat limited discussion of the first three verses of the passage.

Verse 7 reads: "The end of all things is at hand; therefore keep sane and sober for your prayers." This verse is important in the structure of the letter as a whole as it expresses Peter's expectancy of the return of Christ in the near future. Peter was not alone in this expectation. It was a mark of the thinking of many of the New Testament writers. Lumby, in his comments on this verse in the *Expositor's Bible,* lists the following references to show the way in which other New Testament writers shared this expectation: Paul (Phil. 4:15), James (5:8), the writer of Hebrews (10:37), and John (1 John 2:18), page 713. These selections are interesting but by no means exhaustive. The expectancy

of the return of Christ is not as urgent in 1 Peter as it is in Paul's
first letter to the Thessalonians. Peter urges his readers to maintain
sanity and sobriety in their expectation of the return of Christ. We
can understand the need for this advice if we read Second Thessalonians and see what the distortion of Paul's teaching on this
subject did to some of the Thessalonians. We should all live in
this present world in such a manner that we are ready for the
end of life in the world we know if and when it comes to us.
But we must also face seriously our responsibilities in the context
of our contemporary society.

Peter emphasizes again the importance of love of the brethren
as he says: "Above all hold unfailing your love for one another."
The reader is referred to 1 Peter 1:8, 1:22, and 3:8 for the emphasis on love in this brief epistle. Peter adds at this time the
comment that love covers a multitude of sins. The exact meaning
of this comment is not clear. Peter certainly does not mean that
love for people is to be taken as a substitute for the response to
the preaching of the gospel in repentance, faith, love, and obedience. But it is true that, when we are dealing with other people
or they are dealing with us, the certainty of mutual love can
enable us to overlook many of the failures which may mark our
conduct. We can remember that when Jesus sought to restore
Peter to his place as leader of the apostles the one question that
Jesus persistently put to him was the question: "Do you love
me?" (John 21:15-19).

Verse 9 reads: "Practice hospitality ungrudgingly to one
another." Peter lays on his readers the responsibility of practicing
Christian hospitality. The practice of hospitality does not mean
for Peter the giving of feasts. Peter is thinking of the reception,
entertainment, and relief of travelers, particularly of Christian
travelers going from one church to another. The practice ungrudgingly of hospitality was an important Christian virtue in the world
in which Peter lived. Other New Testament references to it are
Romans 12:13; 1 Timothy 3:2; 5:11; Titus 1:8; and 3 John 5.
Bigg comments on this verse: "Indeed without a liberal practice
of this virtue the mission of the church would have been impos-

sible" (*St. Peter and St. Jude,* p. 173). In the time of Jonathan
Edwards his wife, Sarah, in addition to caring for their large
family, did a remarkable job of furnishing sleeping places and
meals to the preachers who came to them (See *Married to a
Difficult Man*, Dodds.) And as the church in America sought to
follow the people as the frontier moved west, the Methodist
circuit riders received very small salaries but expected and received
hospitality from the people they served.

The basic idea of verse 10 is that God in his grace has given
to us various gifts and that we are to use them in our ministry
to each other as good stewards of God's varied grace. The verse
that follows gives us some idea of what Peter had in mind. He
refers here to the gift of speaking. His mind goes back to the
various oracles which would be familiar to his readers. We are
not to think that Peter would have any sympathy with the pattern
of going to pagan oracles of gods that Peter himself did not
believe to exist. But the idea of these oracles was that a human
being became the instrument of the revelation of the will of the
god. Peter transfers this to the Christian faith with the idea of
individuals entering in by study, meditation, and the guidance of
the Spirit to the meaning of the Scriptures until they could be the
bearer of this meaning to others. We have today the witness to
Jesus Christ as it is found in the New Testament, and Christian
witness should be the effort to understand this testimony in its
relevance to life situations today. Peter thinks also of the rendering
of service. Jesus came not to be ministered unto but to minister,
and the Christians should seek in his name to minister to each
other and to human beings in need wherever they find them.
God's gifts are varied. We do not all have the same gifts but we
are to use the gifts we have in a ministry in which we look to
God for strength. We do not distort Peter's meaning when we
think both of natural gifts and acquired gifts. The work of the
church today requires various talents. Those who are qualified to
do so can serve the church in a ministry of music. And Peter
in his ministry in Jerusalem was familiar with a situation in which
for a time much of the time of the apostles had to be given to

serving tables. The first deacons were chosen to relieve the apostles of other duties that they might give themselves to prayer and the ministry of the word (Acts 6:4).

This passage from Peter is similar to a passage from Paul in which he says: "Having gifts that differ according to the grace given to us, let us use them: if prophecy, in proportion to our faith; if service, in our serving; he who teaches, in his teaching; he who exhorts, in his exhortation; he who contributes, in liberality; he who gives aid, with zeal; he who does acts of mercy, with cheerfulness" (Romans 12:6-7). And in Ephesians we have a similar passage. We have looked at part of this passage as we have thought of the Christ as he descended into the lower parts of the earth. But in the same passage there is the thought of the Christ who is ascended into heaven and has given gifts unto men. In Ephesians 4:11 we read: "And his gifts were that some should be apostles, some prophets, some evangelists, some pastors and teachers." These gifts which vary with individuals are all given for the work of the building up of the body of Christ. It is interesting to notice that neither in this passage, or in the passage we quoted from Romans, or in the letter of Peter do we find any reference to the gift of tongues which Paul deals with in the fourteenth chapter of First Corinthians. Neither do we find in these passages any reference to the gifts of working miracles as signs of the presence of God and the integrity of the message. Paul does refer to this in Romans 15:18-19, and Acts witnesses dramatically to the early church's memory of Peter's experience of the miraculous. Perhaps it is significant however, that Peter does not mention it in his letter. Peter is probably thinking primarily of the situation he would find in the churches to which he is writing.

Peter says that God has given us various gifts and that he calls us to be good stewards of them in order that in everything God may be glorified through Jesus Christ. We are reminded here of Paul's statement in 1 Cor. 10:31: "Whether you eat or drink, or whatever you do, do all to the glory of God." In the answer to the first question of the Westminster Shorter Catechism we read: "Man's chief end is to glorify God." Peter closes the passage we are considering with the doxology: "To him belong glory and dominion for ever and ever. Amen." Scholars are agreed that the *him* in this statement points to Jesus Christ, and that Peter is thus saying that eternal glory and dominion characterize the continuing life and reign of Christ. It is almost impossible to imagine how Peter could have spoken more emphatically about the significance of Jesus Christ for our faith today.

15

The Fiery Trial

"Do not be surprised at the fiery ordeal
which comes upon you to prove you, as
though something strange were happening
to you." 1 Peter 4:12

Scripture Background: 1 Peter 4:12-19

In this passage Peter returns to the central theme which has
been woven into the epistle as a whole. Although Peter in his
letter says many things on many subjects, his original concern
in writing the letter is to prepare the Christians in the provinces
of the Roman Empire in Asia to face the sufferings which he
knew would come to them in the light of their faith. Peter will
refer again to this theme in the last chapter of the letter. But as
he writes this portion of the fourth chapter he seems to be aware
of a peculiar time of testing which the Christians of Asia were
about to experience. The Christians in Rome, who possibly included Peter, in the early part of 64 A.D. must have been aware
of the increasing tensions with those who were not Christian
that were to find expression in the Neronian persecutions. This
situation in Rome would not directly affect the Christians in
Asia. We do not know what the fiery trial was, but the best
guess would be that it was Peter's expectation of the beginning
of serious persecutions for the Christians in Asia.

When Peter speaks of the fiery ordeal that is coming on the
Christians of Asia, he is going back to his reference to suffering
in chapter 1, verse 7. Peter is saying again that, just as metals are
purified by being subjected to intense heat, the genuineness of
the faith of the Christians in Asia will be tested by the ordeal
through which they will pass.

As we do not know the exact nature of the ordeal which the Christians of Asia were facing we can say that the fiery trial can be any experience which is used of God to test the genuineness of our faith. It could be persecution for righteousness. It could be an experience of sickness with the suffering that often goes with it. It could be the suffering that comes to us because of our concern for a person we love. We should not be surprised when in the experiences which life brings to us we face various forms of suffering. These experiences can test our faith. We must accept the difficult things that life brings to us. Experiences of suffering, if we face them as children of God and accept them as part of God's loving purposes for us, even if we do not fully understand that purpose, can be used of God to deepen our faith. And we can rejoice that in this way we are sharing the sufferings of Christ.

Peter distinguishes between the suffering of Christians as part of the discipline of God for them and the suffering that comes as the consequence of doing evil. Peter writes to the Christians of Asia: "Let none of you suffer as a murderer, or a thief, or a wrongdoer, or a mischief-maker." As I write I am thinking of an experience which happened recently in Richmond, Virginia, where I live. A man got so involved in an argument with another man that he went to his home and shot and killed him. When the police closed in on him he tried to take his own life. The shot which he fired in his attempt at suicide did not kill him but it left him permanently blind. He was tried and sentenced to prison for life. When I think of what this man now faces I cannot fail to have compassion on him as a human being who did wrong and will reap the consequences of his sins for life. But I cannot say that this kind of suffering is suffering as a Christian. We live in a world that is filled with evil and much of the suffering of that world comes as the consequences of wrong doing. But Peter is writing to Christians and to them he writes: "If one suffers as a Christian, let him not be ashamed, but under that name let him glorify God" (1 Peter 4:16).

It is in this setting that Peter writes: "The time has come for judgment to begin with the household of God" (1 Peter 4:17).

Peter means that in the providence of God there are situations in which a time of testing comes upon a church. And he would have us believe that in such an experience the church may be tested and purified. This was true of course in the life of the early church. In the beginning of the proclamation of the gospel there were times in which the church grew very rapidly. People joined the church from mixed motives. In the times of persecution the church was purified. Those who were not willing to suffer for their faith dropped out. It was a church that had been purified by many persecutions that finally became so strong that it could not be crushed even by the Roman Empire.

In our own time we have seen a major testing of the church by the rise of Marxism on a world scale. In the days of the student volunteer movement as the major organization for finding candidates for the task of world missions, the slogan of the movement was "The evangelization of the world in this generation." Fifty years ago it seemed an appropriate slogan. The Christian church had been planted in germ at least in most of the nations of the earth. The advocates of Christian missions looked forward to a time in the not too distant future when the Christian church would be established as a dominant force in all of the nations of the world. The reality of the present situation is sobering. Over the vast area covered by the Soviet Union, the church is tolerated but not permitted to interfere with the state or to enter upon a program of active and crusading efforts to present the claims of the gospel on the lives of individuals. Christians are permitted to meet together for worship but not to carry on a vigorous program of youth work and Christian education. In Communist China, which contains perhaps a fourth of the human race, a similar situation prevails. In the emerging nations of Africa it is becoming increasingly difficult to combine a truly ecumenical Christianity with the strong emphasis on nationalism that is promoted by the heads of the local governments. The change which has taken place has come within the lifetime of the writer. Has it come because the churches of America and Europe were too closely tied in with the imperialism of the West? Do we live in a day when the judgment of God has begun with the church? We need also to face the fact that both in America and in Europe a vast secularism has permeated modern society, a secularism in which the basic presuppositions of a Christians society are no longer assumed. Is this another case of judgment beginning at the house of God?

It is in this setting in which Peter contemplates the judgment that begins at the house of God that Peter asks another great question. The question is that if judgment begins at the house of God, "What will be the fate of those who do not obey the gospel of God?" Peter is still thinking primarily of the mystery of suffering. He can speak a word of hope for those who suffer as Christians. But what of those who do not obey the gospel of God as they face the mystery of suffering? Those who do not obey the gospel do not have in the time of suffering the support of those who believe in a moral order which grounds in God. They do not have the support of being part of a community of faith that stands with them and strengthens them. They do not have the support of those who believe in the reality of the presence of the Christ with his people and the support of the Christian hope that beyond the limited time of suffering there is the expectation of an eternal redemption. To the Christians Peter can write at the close of the chapter: "Therefore let those who suffer according to God's will do right and entrust their souls to a faithful Creator" (1 Peter 4:19).

But what shall we say about those who obey not the gospel? We have thought of them as individuals who do not have the sources of comfort that are available to Christians. But what about whole societies where the leaders reject the transcendent authority of moral law, and have no patience with a way of life determined by Jesus and set forth in the letters of Paul and the testimony of Peter? There is no easy answer to this. However, the disintegration of life which is found today in Russia as pictured by Solzhenitsyn gives us an insight. His description helps us to understand that a people cannot reject all of the insights of the Christian faith and expect to achieve a society in which there is respect for the dignity of man, integrity and efficiency, and genuine compassion for those in need.

16
The Exhortation to the Elders

"I exhort the elders among you, as a fellow elder and a witness of the sufferings of Christ as well as a partaker of the glory that is to be revealed." 1 Peter 5:1

Scripture Background: 1 Peter 5:1-5

In connection with our study of Peter's description of the sufferings of Christ on the cross, we have given some attention to his statement in 5:1 that he was an eyewitness of these sufferings. There is some question as to what he means when he says that he exhorts the elders as a partaker of the glory that is to be revealed. Selwyn in commenting on this passage thinks that we may have here a veiled reference to the transfiguration. Interestingly, this is brought out in 2 Peter 1:16-18. Selwyn's interpretation is possible as the vision which Peter received at the time of the transfiguration was a vision of the glory of Jesus as he was telling his disciples of the necessity of his suffering. But Peter in the letter as a whole consistently associates the suffering of Jesus or his followers with the hope of the glory that is to follow. This is stated very clearly in 1 Peter 5:10. The particular way in which we interpret this reference is not vital to the interpretation of our passage as a whole.

Peter says that he writes as a fellow elder to the elders who are among his readers. The letter as a whole is written in Peter's authority as an apostle of Jesus Christ (1 Peter 1:1). But in the passage before us he writes as a fellow elder to the elders in the various churches. That Peter writes to the elders in this way is significant not only in terms of the things he says but also in terms of his recognition of the organization and structure of the church at the time that he was writing. We know of course that as Paul and Barnabas were retracing their steps for brief visits with the churches that had come into being through the response to their preaching on the first missionary journey, they appointed elders in every church (Acts 14:23). We know also that when the issues which were raised by this first missionary journey in which the gospel was offered to the Gentiles were being debated in the church at Jerusalem, the decisions which were made represented the apostles and the *elders* and that the letter which was sent to the Gentile churches was signed by the apostles and the *elders*. (See Acts 15:6 and 22.) A similar pattern of structure was found in the churches of Asia. When Paul was on his final trip to Jerusalem he asked the elders of the church at Ephesus to meet him at Miletus. It is clear also that at this stage in the life of the church the words elder or bishop were used as having essentially the same meaning. (See Titus 1:5-7.) (See also Philemon 1:1 and 1 Timothy 3:1-7 for a statement of the qualifications of bishops and 1 Tim. 3:8-13 for the deacons.)

It is interesting to observe that Peter quietly assumes the same pattern of organization for the churches of Asia who were to receive his letter. In time, of course, the elders became widely known as bishops, and they were made overseers of the organization of the church. A pattern of apostolic succession developed in which the whole life of the church centered in the bishop of Rome. It is not our purpose here to discuss the wisdom of the organizational structure of the church which finally developed. We can observe, however, that there is no sign of this or of other forms of extensive church government in 1 Peter.

At the time of the Reformation the question inevitably arose as to how the church was to be structured. Luther structured the churches he founded so that the princes of Germany were to be acknowledged as the head of the church within their own dominions. Calvin could not do this because the king of France was Catholic. Calvin went back to the persecuted church of the New Testament and set up a pattern of church organization in which the local churches were governed by elders elected by the people. John Knox followed Calvin with a church organization in Scotland in which the people governed themselves through elders elected by the local congregations. Even as this developed, the government by bishops continued in other areas. All of this is very familiar to us now, but in the time of Knox and Calvin these were revolutionary ideas. One remarkable result, however, was that as the Scotch and the Scotch-Irish moved from their island homes to settle in various portions of our earth, they actually carried with them a pattern of organization which owed its inspiration to that of the persecuted church of the New Testament.

Peter's charge to the elders can be summed up in his statement: "Tend the flock of God that is your charge" (1 Peter 5:2). The congregations in which they seek to carry on their ministry do not belong to them. They are the flock of God. As Peter gives this charge we are reminded of the charge which Jesus gave to Peter when Peter after his denial was restored to his position as leader of the apostles. Peter was charged with the work of feeding the sheep and tending the sheep. It could be that Peter wrote his letter to the churches of Asia as a fullfillment in part of Christ's charge to him. (See John 21:15-17.) Peter does not elaborate his charge, but he speaks three words of warning to the elders concerning temptations that might come to them as they discharged their responsibilities. They were to do their work not by constraint but willingly. They were not to do their work for what he calls shameful gain. The reference is probably to receiving money from the church for the things they do. Paul deals with this matter much more fully in 1 Corinthians 9:1-18 and 2 Corinthians 12:13-15. There is a place for financial compensation in the service of the church if this is necessary. But this should never be the central concern of church officers or leaders as they carry on their ministry. Peter is aware too of the subtle temptation to dominate over others as the elder is lifted into positions of leadership. The history of the church will show that Peter's warning against domineering was wisely spoken. The church leader should certainly set an example in personal life. It has been said that we teach some by what we say, more by what we do, and most by what we are. Peter proceeds to make a promise to the elders who are faithful in their discharge of the responsibilities committed to them. He says: "And when the chief Shepherd is manifested you will obtain the unfading crown of glory" (1 Peter 5:4). Here we have another incidental reference to the early church's expectation of the return of Christ in the not too distant future. However, the focus of the verse is really on the idea of reward from Christ for faithful service.

Verse 5 opens with an interesting injunction. Peter writes: "Likewise you that are younger be subject to the elders." In dealing with the structure of the church Peter goes back to the basic principle which he laid down in chapter 2, verse 13, as he says: "Be subject for the Lord's sake to every human institution." Peter would say that those who are not elders should be subject to the elders of the church "for the Lord's sake." While opportunities for changing unjust social and economic relations must be taken, this is a pattern in which we should face many of the relationships of life. This is true whether we are thinking of the state or of the economic order or the home or of the relationships involved in the structure of the church. It is in this setting that Peter writes to the elders: "Clothe yourselves, all of you, with humility towards one another, for 'God opposes the proud, but gives grace to the humble.' " This passage is put in quotation marks in the Revised Standard Version because it goes back to Proverbs 3:34. Peter does not quote accurately, but in his own language he expresses a great insight. He says that God resists the proud. The man who is acting in pride will find that God is resisting him but the man who is walking in humility will find that God is giving to him his grace.

17

Freedom from Anxiety

"Cast all your anxieties on him, for he cares about you." 1 Peter 5:7

Scripture Background: 1 Peter 5:6-11

Peter follows his message to the elders with a word of advice to all of his readers. He says to them: "Humble yourselves therefore under the mighty hand of God, that in due time he may exalt you" (1 Peter 5:6). This is a conclusion that follows naturally from his closing word to the elders when he says: "Clothe yourselves, all of you, with humility toward one another, for 'God opposes the proud, but gives grace to the humble.' " The basis of all genuine humility is the recognition of the mighty hand of God. Peter's statement is almost a promise. He would have his readers believe that those who humble themselves in recognition of the mighty power of God will in time experience a divine lifting up. The God who gives grace to the humble will give them the capacity to be adequate to the tasks to which he calls them. He can also give them a sense of the dignity and purpose of their human existence. This can deliver them from a defeatist type of self-depreciation without leading them to the sin of pride.

It is in this setting that Peter places the verse which is central to our passage. He writes to his readers: "Cast all your anxieties on *him,* for he cares for you" (1 Peter 5:7). The pronoun, him, in this verse refers to God. It goes back to Peter's reference to the mighty hand of God. We could, of course, think of casting our cares on the Christ who loves us. But Peter is saying that the God who has made himself known in Jesus

Christ is the God upon whom we can cast all of our anxieties in our confidence both of his power and his care for us. It is difficult for us to believe that the God of the universe cares for us as individuals. But this is the God that Jesus reveals to us. He is the God who has the capacity for the minute and the seemingly unimportant. Jesus has said to us: "Are not two sparrows sold for a penny? And not one of them will fall to the ground without your father's will. But even the hairs of your head are all numbered. Fear not, therfore; you are of more value than many sparrows" (Matt. 10:29-31). He has pictured God as the Father waiting for the return of the prodigal son (Luke 15:11-32).

The pattern of freedom from anxieties to which Peter calls his readers can be a mark of vital Christian living. Paul writes to the Philippians: "Have no anxiety about anything, but in everything by prayer and supplication with thanksgiving let your requests be made known to God. And the peace of God, which passes all understanding, will keep your hearts and your minds in Christ Jesus." And Paul also says to the Philippians: "And my God will supply every need of yours according to his riches in glory in Christ Jesus" (Philippians 4:6-7, 19).

Jesus himself gives an invitation to discipleship which involves a promise of freedom from anxiety. He says: "Come to me, all who labor and are heavy laden, and I will give you rest. Take my yoke upon you, and learn from me; for I am gentle and lowly in heart, and you will find rest for your souls. For my yoke is easy, and my burden is light" (Matt. 11:28-30). We should notice that his call is addressed to those who are weary and are heavy laden, and that the response to it involves the taking up of a yoke. Jesus refers to himself when he says "I am gentle and lowly in heart." Peter had learned the lesson of humility from Jesus. And the promise of this invitation is that those who respond to it will find rest for their souls. It is important that in the Gospel of John the words spoken by Jesus on the night when he knows he is to be arrested concern freedom from anxiety and fear. In this situation Jesus says to his disciples: "Peace I leave with you; my peace I give to you. . . . Let not your hearts be troubled, neither let them be afraid" (John 14:27). And in the close of the sixteenth chapter he says: "In the world you have tribulation; but be of good cheer, I have overcome the world" (verse 33).

Peter's message to his readers in which he urges them to cast all of their anxieties on God in the knowledge that God cares for them is followed by a verse which at first glance seems to be a strange verse with which to follow his advice. He writes to them in verse 8: "Be sober, be watchful. Your adversary the devil prowls around like a roaring lion, seeking some one to devour." But this verse fits into the pattern of tension similar to that which marks the sayings of Jesus as he calls his disciples to inner peace. The conceptual background here resembles the picture of Satan in Job as he is going to and fro on the earth (Job 1:7). And the comparison of the devil to a roaring lion seeking someone to devour would have been understood by Peter's readers as some of them may have lived in situations in which they were in danger from man-eating lions. Peter probably believed in a personal devil. We can be reasonably sure that Jesus shared this belief. Consider for example the word of Jesus to Peter: "Simon, Simon, behold, Satan demanded to have you, that he might sift you like wheat, but I have prayed for you that your faith may not fail" (Luke 22:31). There is no easy answer to the mystery of evil in our world, and the simple biblical assumptions of evil spirits and a personal devil may be as satisfactory as other patterns of dealing with the problem. But regardless of the ways in which we may interpret this belief in the existence of a personal devil, no one who looks out on our world today can deny the tremendous reality of evil in our world. Peter knows that his readers are living in a world in which they are surrounded by evil. There is the evil which is outside of us and the evil that exists within us. And it is in this situation that Peter has called his readers to be sober and watchful and to resist the suggestions of evil as those who are firm in the faith.

Like us, Peter's readers face a world in which they are aware of the depths of evil and in which they know personal experiences of suffering. In returning to this theme Peter is going back in his closing remarks to the theme which has been central in his letter as a whole. Peter reminds his readers that in facing the experiences of suffering which he knows will come to them they are in no way unique. They can know that similar experience of suffering are required of their brotherhood throughout the world. We can set Peter's words in the setting of the experiences of Christians in the midst of our contemporary world as they face times of testing and suffering. Peter says to his readers: "And after you have suffered a little while, the God of all grace, who has called you to his eternal glory in Christ, will himself restore, establish, and strengthen you" (1 Peter 5:10). Peter reminds his readers that in contrast to the ultimate hope of eternal glory in Christ their suffering is for a little while. Paul makes the same contrast as he writes to the Corinthians: "This slight momentary affliction is preparing for us an eternal weight of glory beyond all comparison" (2 Cor. 4:17). Peter also makes the positive statement: "The God of all grace... has called you to his eternal glory in Christ." This is as true of believing Christians today as it was of the readers to whom Peter was addressing his letter. The God of all grace is still calling those who respond in faith to the proclamation of the gospel to their eternal glory in Christ Jesus.

In commenting on the last part of verse 10 where Peter tells his readers that the God of all grace will restore, establish, and strengthen them, Selwyn writes: "What Peter gives his readers is not a prayer but a promise" (*The First Epistle of Peter*, p. 240).

The promise is followed by a doxology. But the doxology is not unrelated to the promise. As he is speaking of the God of all grace who has called us to his eternal glory in Christ Jesus and has promised to restore, establish, and strengthen us, Peter says: "To him be the dominion for ever and ever. Amen." We are not called upon to commit ourselves in faith to a God who is without the will and the power to accomplish his purposes in us and keep his promises to us. Peter says that the God to whom he bears testimony is the God to whom there has been given dominion for ever and ever. He is the God who has dominion within our contemporary society and the God who will continue to have dominion for ever and ever. When Peter tells us to cast all of our anxieties upon the God who cares for us, he is writing in the midst of a world in which he knows that his readers will have to face the power of evil, the reality of suffering, and the certainty of death. But he knows that the God who has come to us in Christ will have dominion for ever and ever.

18
Silvanus and Greetings

"Silvanus, a faithful brother." 1 Peter 5:12

"She who is at Babylon . . . sends you greetings; and so does my son Mark. Greet one another with the kiss of love. . . . Peace to all of you that are in Christ." 1 Peter 5: 13-14

Scripture Background: 1 Peter 5: 13-14

The closing verses tell us that the letter has been written by Silvanus, whom Peter describes as a faithful brother. The Silvanus who is mentioned here has been traditionally identified with the Silas who was the companion of Paul on his second missionary journey. As such he was also associated with Paul and Timothy in the letters to the Thessalonians (1 Thess. 1:1 and 2 Thess. 1:1). And in both letters he is called Silvanus. It could be the case of a single individual being known by both names, for Silvanus has been regarded as a Latin form of the name Silas.

In this respect, we note that in Acts Silas is portrayed as a significant figure among the personalities of the New Testament period. He was selected along with a man named Judas but called Barsabbas to be the actual bearers of the letter from the Jerusalem Council to the church at Antioch. They are chosen as leading men among the brethren in Jerusalem. Silas had probably been with the church at Jerusalem from the beginning. After they had read the letter to the church at Antioch we are told that Judas and Silas who were themselves prophets exhorted the brethren with many words and strengthened them (Acts 15:32). We would conclude from this statement that Silas was a Christian leader who had been given the gift of prophecy. When Paul and Barnabas disagreed over the taking of John Mark as an attendant on the second missionary journey, Paul separated from Barnabas and chose Silas as his companion. Silas was with Paul in the brief imprisonment at Philippi and joined with Paul in praying and singing of hymns to God when they were fastened with their feet in the stocks in the inner prison (Acts 16:25). We learn from this story that Silas was also a Roman citizen. We would judge from the passages of Acts written in the first person plural (the "we" passages of Acts) that Luke joined Paul and Silas at Troas and was with them in the experience at Phillipi. This would mean that Luke and Silas knew each other. We do not need to follow all of the movements of Silas but we do know that he was with Paul at Thessalonica and also at Corinth.

The close association of Silas with Paul and the broad link between Silvanus/Silas and Peter is very suggestive with respect to the basic unity of the thought of the early church. Balancing the diversity, the general compatability of beliefs found expression through these traditions and portraits of personal ties. In commenting on the authorship of 1 Peter, Selwyn writes: "It was the joint work of Silvanus and St. Peter, the former supplying the literary composition, much of it gathered from the common tradition, the latter providing the Apostolic testimony to the underlying facts of the Gospel and their application to the readers' condition" (*The First Epistle of Peter,* p. 242).

Peter says to his readers: "I have written briefly to you, exhorting and declaring that this is the true grace of God; stand fast in it" (1 Peter 5:12). This points up both the purpose and the brevity of the letter. Limited to five chapters, it is a declaration of the true grace of God and an exhortation to its readers to hear its message and to stand fast in their response to it. This summary can be Peter's message to those who read his letter today as it is translated in a language that was not even in existence when Peter wrote.

The letter closes with a series of greetings. The first is: "She who is at Babylon, who is likewise chosen, sends you greetings." The expression "She who is at Babylon" is a correct translation of the Greek text. But what does it mean? There have been some who say that the person referred to was Peter's wife. Most commentators reject this and believe that the reference is to the church at Babylon. The Latin Vulgate translates it this way. What is the meaning of the reference to Babylon? The great majority of commentators believe that the word Babylon is a veiled reference to Rome. Selwyn reminds us that "Rome is called Babylon in Revelation 17 and 18." He adds that "it does not appear to be used there for the first time" (*The First Epistle of Peter*, p. 243). In this pattern Rome is given the name of Babylon as the great enemy of the people of God. When we remember the agony that characterized the period of the Neronian persecutions, we can fully understand this use of the word. And the phrase "who is likewise chosen" fits this interpretation. From this perspective, Peter is telling the Christians in Asia that God has also called into being a significant community of faith in Rome. If this interpretation of Peter's letter is correct it does give support to the view that Peter may have been in Rome at the time the letter was written. At the least, it confirms the tradition of Peter's association with Rome. This greeting from the church at Rome reminds us of the greetings which frequently come from the churches in persecuted lands today. It could be the greeting of Johannes Hamel as he writes of Serving God in East Germany or the greetings from our Christian brethren in Czechoslovakia or in Hungary. It could also be the greetings which come from behind the Iron Curtain of Russia or the Bamboo Curtain of China.

Peter adds: "And so does my son, Mark." The reference is of course to John Mark. Peter is thinking of John Mark as his son in the faith. John Mark was the son of a sister of Barnabas named Mary who had a home in Jerusalem (Acts 12:12). It was to this house that Peter went after his miraculous deliverance from the hands of Herod, the King. Mark started with Barnabas and Paul on the first missionary journey. But Mark turned back after they had reached the mainland of Asia and returned to Jerusalem (Acts 13:13). In the planning of the second missionary journey Barnabas wanted to give Mark, his nephew, a second chance. But Paul would not agree. There is evidence in Paul's letters to show that he changed his opinion of Mark. He writes to the Colossians:

"Aristarchus, my fellow prisoner, salutes you, and Mark, the cousin of Barnabas (concerning whom you have received instructions—if he comes to you, receive him)" (Colossians 4:10). And in the closing section of 2 Timothy, Paul writes to Timothy: "Get Mark and bring him with you; for he is very useful in serving me" (2 Timothy 4:11).

The reference of Peter, as at the close of his letter he includes the greeting of Mark whom he calls his son in the faith, is important. There was a tradition in the church that Mark wrote the Gospel which bears his name and that he depended in the main on the information which he had received from Peter's preaching. The reader is referred to the commentary by Bigg for an able summary of this tradition (*St. Peter and St. Jude,* p. 82). Both Matthew and Luke depended heavily on the Gospel of Mark when they wrote their Gospels. This means that the early Christians felt quite indebted to Peter for much of the written record which is preserved for us in the first three Gospels.

In the last verse of the letter Peter writes: "Greet one another with the kiss of love." Paul closes a number of his letters with the injunction: "Greet one another with a holy kiss" (Romans 16:16; 1 Cor. 16:20; 2 Cor. 13:12; 1 Thess. 5:26). Paul believed in this salutation between Christians but he wanted to be sure it was a *holy* kiss. Apparently this custom was circumspectly observed as an expression of Christian love. And Peter gives his final greeting to the Christians of Asia and to us as he writes: "Peace to all of you that are in Christ."

19
The Creed of Peter

We can hear the Apostle Peter speak to us today by bringing together and developing some of the traditions which the church has long associated with his teachings. In doing this, we can hear him say:

I am Simon Peter, apostle of Jesus Christ.

I believe in the God who has made himself known as the Father of our Lord Jesus Christ as the one and the only, the true and the living God. I believe that he is the sovereign Lord who made the heaven, and the earth and the sea and everything in them (Acts 4:24).

I believe that Jesus is the Christ, the Son of the living God (Matthew 16:16). I believe with Paul that he was designated Son of God in power according to the Spirit of holiness by his resurrection from the dead (Romans 1:4). I believe that there is no other name under heaven given among men by which we must be saved (Acts 4:12).

I believe in the Holy Spirit as God present in the hearts of people, witnessing to the truth of the gospel proclamation and enabling those who give themselves in repentance, and love, faith, and obedience to Jesus Christ to live holy lives (1 Peter 1:2, 12). I express my faith through Paul's benediction: "The grace of the Lord Jesus Christ and the love of God and the fellowship of the Holy Spirit be with you all" (2 Cor. 13:14). I believe in the unity of God and in the existence of this one God as Father, Son, and Holy Spirit.

I was with Jesus in the days of his flesh as he went about doing good (Acts 10:38). I heard his teachings and witnessed his healing ministry and his mighty works. I believe that he committed no sin and that no guile was found on his lips (1 Peter 2:22). I know that he was rejected by his own people and put to death by crucifixion. He was buried in a tomb. I believe that on the morning of the third day after his death God raised him from the dead, and gave him glory (1 Peter 1:21). I heard the message of the women concerning the empty tomb. I stood on the outside of the tomb and saw that the stone had been rolled away. I entered the tomb and found it empty with the grave clothes laid aside (John 20:28). I was among the first of those to whom the living Lord manifested himself alive after his passion (Luke 24:34: 1 Cor. 15:5). On several occasions I was with the disciples when the risen Jesus made himself known to them. I was also with a larger group of his followers to whom he appeared (1 Cor. 15:6). I believe that Jesus is now in heaven at the right hand of God with angels, authorities, and powers subject to him (1 Peter 3:22).

I believe that Jesus died in fulfillment of the purpose of the Father in heaven to send his Son to die for the sins of the world (Romans 8:32). I believe that his death was accepted by the Father as atonement for the sins of those for whom he died and that on the basis of what Jesus Christ has done for us the forgiveness of sins is offered to all who will receive it. I believe that those who put their trust in him will receive from him the capacity to become children of God and the expectancy of an eternal redemption either at the time of their death or at the time of his return (1 Peter 1:9, 21; 5:4, 10).

I believe in the church as the community of those who because of their knowledge of the resurrection world of God as it has confronted them in Jesus Christ have become strangers and pilgrims in the context of the society in which they are now living (1 Peter 2:11). I believe that the church is the community of those who at one time were not a people but have now become the community of God's people. I believe that membership in this community is open to all who will acknowledge Jesus Christ as Lord and Savior (1 Peter 2:9-10).

I believe that God's purpose is for those who are in this community to declare the wonderful works of him who called them out of darkness into his marvelous light (1 Peter 2:9). I believe that those who are in the new community of faith are called upon to be witnesses to Jesus to all peoples and to continue this witness until the return of their Lord. I believe that those who move out in obedience to his command to witness will know the mystical presence of the Christ, a presence that is unseen but not unreal and that Jesus will give them through the presence of his Spirit with them power to be adequate to the tasks to which he sets them (Matt. 28:18-20; Acts 1:8).

I believe that Christians should seek within the context of this present world to live lives of love for the brethren and also of love for those who call them enemies and persecute them (1 Peter 1:22; 3:8-9). I believe also that Christians should walk in a way of life marked by a concern for holiness and in a pattern of humility in which they may in time know a divine lifting up (1 Peter 3:6).

I believe that Christians must face various trials, which may include suffering and persecution, in the knowledge of the sufferings of Christ and as part of their fellowship in his sufferings and their certainty of the glory that comes at the end of their pilgrimage.

I believe in the union of one man and one woman in a marriage relation in which they mutually accept the responsibilities as well as the privileges of marriage and seek to live together in this life as those who know that they are heirs together of eternal life.

I believe that Christians should take their proper place in the institutions of the society in which they live whether they be in the economic order or in the pattern of government. But I would affirm that they should never forget that they are part of the new community of God's people. I know that as they seek to know the will of God for them in the situations they actually face they may find that their loyalty to Jesus Christ sets them in tension with many of the patterns of their society. I know that the risen Lord at the time of his ascension told us that it was not for us to know the time or the seasons which the Father had fixed by his own power. I know also that he laid on us the responsibility of witnessing to him to the most distant places on the earth and to the end of the age (Acts 1:6-8; Matt. 28:20). I shared with the other apostles the hope that the Lord would return in the near future (1 Peter 4:7). I did not feel that the delay in his coming affected my responsibility to live in such a manner that I would be ready for him if he came (Matt. 24:44). I knew also through the word of·the risen Lord to me that I would not live until the time of his return and that my way to the realization of his presence in the resurrection world of God would be through a martyr's death (John 21:18-19).

I believe that in everything God is glorified through Jesus Christ and that to Jesus Christ belong glory and dominion for ever and ever. Amen (1 Peter 4:11).